A Practical Guide to the
COMMODITIES
MARKETS

Ronald C. Spurga

Prentice-Hall, Inc., Englewood Cliffs, New Jersey 07632

Library of Congress Cataloging in Publication Data

Spurga, Ronald C.
   A practical guide to the commodites markets.

   Includes index.
   1. Commodity exchanges.   I. Title.
HG6046.S66   1983   332.64'4   82-12299
ISBN 0-13-690644-3
ISBN 0-13-690636-2 (pbk.)

This book is offered for sale with the understanding that the author is not engaged in legal or accounting services. The author specifically disclaims any liability, loss, or risk, personal or otherwise, that is incurred as a consequence, directly or indirectly, of the use and application of any of the contents of this work.

Printed in the United States of America

This book is available at a special discount when ordered
in bulk quantities. Contact Prentice-Hall, Inc., General
Publishing Division, Special Sales, Englewood Cliffs, N.J. 07632.

Editorial/production supervision: Marlys Lehmann
Cover design © 1983 by Jeannette Jacobs
Manufacturing buyer: Pat Mahoney

ISBN 0-13-690644-3

ISBN 0-13-690636-2 {PBK.}

Prentice-Hall International, Inc., *London*
Prentice-Hall of Australia Pty. Limited, *Sydney*
Prentice-Hall Canada Inc., *Toronto*
Prentice-Hall of India Private Limited, *New Delhi*
Prentice-Hall of Japan, Inc., *Tokyo*
Prentice-Hall of Southeast Asia Pte. Ltd., *Singapore*
Whitehall Books Limited, *Wellington, New Zealand*
Editora Prentice-Hall do Brasil Ltda., *Rio de Janeiro*

For Marie and Kathleen and my mother

Contents

"United Metropolitan Improved Hot Muffin and Crumpet Baking and Punctual Delivery Company. Capital, five million, in five hundred thousand shares of ten pounds each." Why the very name will get the shares up to a premium in ten days.

Charles Dickens
Nicholas Nickleby

I

SHOULD YOU SPECULATE?

1

Guidelines for the Beginning Commodities Speculator

A student of mine once came into class armed with the following statistical information:

Market Yields

	1/8/82 (Noon)
Prime Lending Rate	15.75%
Effective since	12/1/81
Discount Rate at Federal Reserve Bank	12.00
Federal Funds	12.00
Repurchase Agreements	12.00
U.S. Treasury Issues Bills	
3 Months	11.95
6 Months	13.25
1 Year	13.70
Coupons	
2 Years	14.04
4 Years	14.35
7 Years	14.62
10 Years	14.47
Long Bond	14.10
Negotiable Certificates of Deposits—Secondary Market	
1 Month	12.45
2 Months	12.90
6 Months	13.75
1 Year	14.25

Market Yields (*continued*)

	1/8/82 (Noon)
Banker's Acceptances	
1 Month	12.40
3 Months	12.80
6 Months	13.80
Eurodollar Deposits	
1 Month	13.13
2 Months	13.38
3 Months	13.63
Commercial Paper—Prime Names	
Directly placed by:	
Finance Companies	
1 Week	11.75
1 Month	12.25
3 Months	12.25
Bank Holding Companies	
1 Month	11.75
Dealer Placed:	
3 months	12.50
New AA Corporate Utility Bond	17.00
Tax Exempt	
6 Months Project Notes	7.10
1 Year AAA Bond	8.10
5 Year AAA Bond	9.60
20 Year AAA Bond	12.50

This student was confused by the array of financial investments available to him. He knew that a treasury bill (minimum investment $10,000) would yield him approximately 13 percent, whereas certificates of deposit, bankers acceptances, and commercial paper would yield somewhat more, reflecting their high risk. His question to me was: "If I can get thirteen percent by investing in a government obligation, why should I concern myself with other investments?"

My reply to him was simply: "Because the inflation rate is fifteen percent."

We then got into a discussion of equities (common stocks), and we both agreed that the autos, airlines, public utilities, farm equipment manufacturers, and domestic steel manufacturers were slumping badly and that this was a reflection of lagging productivity and increased energy costs in our economy in general. If productivity didn't increase and oil prices decline, equities would continue to be unattractive.

Were there other investment media? The answer is yes, the commodities markets.

This text is designed to outline the operation of those commodities markets and provide a sensible approach to investing in them. Organizationally, the text will deal with the mechanics of futures trading in commodities and, building on this base, guide the careful investor to potential investment opportunities.

2

The Speculator and
the Commodity Exchanges

HISTORY AND ORIGIN

When civilization began, trading started. Bartering for different commodities has probably been done since time immemorial. Coined money appeared sometime between 800 B.C. and 700 B.C. Soon, instead of bartering as a means of business, coined money was used. Eventually trading had to be done on the basis of future delivery, as a merchant would sell out his complete stock but still have customers waiting to buy. The merchant would then take a partial payment and guarantee delivery at a future date. This type of transaction was probably the beginning of the present-day futures contract.

For nearly three hundred years, commodity futures contracts were used. Merchants and processors of food would bid for a farmer's crop, before or after planting. Both parties involved were protected and would not have to fear that drastic price changes of the crop during harvest or delivery would alter the normal course of their business. Today's commodity futures markets still offer this protection.

Commodity Exchanges

What is a commodity exchange? A commodity exchange is an organized market of buyers and sellers of various types of commodities. It is public to the extent that anyone can trade through member firms. It provides a trading place for commodities, regulates the trading practices of the members, gathers and transmits price information, inspects and governs commodities traded on the exchange, supervises warehouses that store the commodity, and provides means for settling disputes between members. All transactions must be conducted in a pit on the exchange floor within certain hours.

Futures Contract

What is a futures contract? A futures contract is a contract between two parties where the buyer agrees to accept delivery at a specified price from the seller of a particular commodity, in a designated month in the future, if it is not liquidated before the contract reaches maturity. A futures contract is not an option; nothing in it is conditional. Each contract calls for a specified amount and grade of product. For example: A person buying a February Pork Belly contract at 52.40 in effect is making a legal obligation, now, to accept delivery of 38,000 pounds of frozen pork bellies, to be delivered during the month of February, for which the buyer will pay 52.40 per pound.

Average traders do not take delivery of a futures contract, since they will normally close out their position before the futures contract matures. As a matter of fact, a survey conducted by a leading exchange has estimated that less than 3 percent of the contracts traded are settled by actual delivery.

Futures contracts are traded on different exchanges. Following is a list of the major exchanges and the type of contracts they trade:

1. BOARD OF TRADE.   Wheat, Corn, Soybeans, Soybean Meal, Soybean Oil, Iced Broilers, Silver (5,000 ounces), Plywood, Oats, Gold, Ginnie Mae's, Commercial Paper, Treasury Bonds, Treasury Notes.

2. CHICAGO MERCANTILE EXCHANGE.   Live Cattle, Fresh Eggs, Live Hogs, Lumber, Russet Potatoes, Pork Bellies, Turkeys, Stud Lumber, Feeder Cattle, Iced Broilers.

3. INTERNATIONAL MONETARY MARKET.   Eight Currencies, Silver Coins, Gold (100 ounces), 90-Day Treasury Bills, One-Year Treasury Bills, Four-Year Treasury Notes.

4. NEW YORK MERCANTILE EXCHANGE.   Platinum, Palladium, Round White Potatoes, Silver Coins, Gold (1 kilo), Gold (400 ounces), Currencies, #2 Heating Oil.

5. COFFEE, SUGAR, AND COCOA EXCHANGE.   Coffee, Sugar, Cocoa.

6. NEW YORK FUTURES EXCHANGE.   20-Year Treasury Bonds, 90-Day Treasury Bills, Five Currencies.

7. COMMODITY EXCHANGE.   Silver (5,000 ounces), Copper (25,000 pounds), Gold (100 ounces), 90-Day Treasury Bills, Ginnie Mae's.

8. NEW YORK COTTON EXCHANGE.   Cotton, Orange Juice, Propane, Gas, Crude Oil.

9. MID AMERICA COMMODITY EXCHANGE.   Grains in units of 1,000 bushels, Silver (1,000 ounces), Silver Coins (five bags, $1,000 each), Gold (1 kilo), Hogs (15,000 pounds), Cattle (20,000 pounds).

THE HEDGER AND SPECULATOR

A hedger buys or sells a futures contract in order to reduce the risk of loss through price variation. A short hedger sells a futures contract to protect the possible decline in the actual commodity owned by him. A long hedger purchases a futures contract to protect the possible advance in the value of an actual commodity needed to be purchased in the future.

The speculator is an important factor in the volume of future trading today. He, in effect, voluntarily assumes the risk, which the hedger tries to avoid with the expectations of making a profit. He is somewhat of an insurance underwriter. The largest number of traders on any commodity exchange is the speculator. In order for the hedger to participate, he must have continuous trading interests and activity in the market. This trading activity stems from the role of the speculator, because he involves himself in buying or selling of futures contracts with the idea of making a profit on the advance or decline of prices. The speculator tries to forecast prices in advance of delivery and is willing to buy or sell on this basis. A speculator involves himself in an inescapable risk.

Can You Be a Speculator?

Now, can you be a speculator? Before considering entering the futures market as a speculator, you should understand several facts about the market and also about yourself. In order to enter into the futures market, you must understand that you are dealing with a margin account. Margins are as low as 5 to 10 percent of the total value of the futures contract, so you are obtaining a greater leverage on your capital.

Fluctuations in price are rapid, volatile, and wide. It is possible to make a very large profit in a short period of time, but it is also possible to take a substantial loss. In fact, surveys taken by the Agricultural Department have shown that up to 95 percent of the individuals speculating in commodity markets have lost money. This does not mean that some of their trades were not profitable, but after a period of time with a given sum of money they ended up being losers.

Taking you as an individual, let us see whether you have the characteristics to become a commodity trader. Number one and the most important is that you do not take money that you have set aside for your future, or money you need daily to support your family or yourself. Number two, and almost equally important, is that you must be willing to assume losses and be willing to assume these losses with such a temperament that it is not going to affect your everyday life. Money used in the futures market should be money that has been set aside for strictly risk purposes, and if this money is not risk capital, your methods of trading could be seriously affected, because you cannot afford to be a loser.

Another very important factor is that you must not feel that you are going to take a thousand, two thousand, five or ten thousand dollars and place this with a brokerage firm and not follow the daily happenings of the market. Price fluctuations are fast, and as stated before, wide, so you must not only be in contact with your account executive daily but know and study the technical facts that may be affecting the particular market in which you are speculating.

The individual who makes his first trade by buying a contract on Monday and selling this contract on the following Wednesday, making six hundred dollars on a thousand-dollar investment in a period of two days, suddenly says to himself, "Where has this market been all my life? Why am I working? Why not just concentrate on this market if every two days or so I can make six hundred dollars?" This is a fallacy. The next trade he will feel confident that because of his first profitable trade the market will always go his way even though he is now showing a loss in his position. He still feels that the market will turn around in his direction. If you become married to a particular commodity futures contract and constantly feel that the losses you are taking at the present time will reverse into profits, you are really fighting the market and in most cases fighting a losing battle. This could lead to disaster. There is a saying that you let your profits ride, but liquidate your losses fast.

If in any way you are uneasy with a position you are holding, it is better to liquidate it. If, prior to the time of buying or selling a contract, you are not sure that this is the right step to take, do not take it. To protect yourself against this hazard, you should decide in advance on every trade and exactly how much you intend to lose.

Another important point is not to involve yourself in too many markets. It is difficult to know all the technical facts and be able to follow numerous markets. In addition, if you are in a winning position, be conservative as to how you add additional contracts or pyramid your position. Being conservative will sometimes cause you to miss certain moves in certain markets and you may feel this to be wrong, but over a long period of time, this conservatism will be profitable to you.

If at this point you feel that you are ready, both financially and mentally, to trade commodities, the next step is to begin the actual mechanics of trading a futures contract.

OPENING AN ACCOUNT

The first important factor is to decide which brokerage firm will afford you the best service. To accomplish this, you should do a little research by checking with the various exchanges about different brokerage firms. You should study their advertising, market letters, and other information. These should all be presented in a businesslike manner and have no unwarranted claims, such as a guarantee of profit without indicating the possibility of loss.

The brokerage firm must be able to handle orders on all commodity exchanges. Do not pick just any account executive in a firm, but one you feel confident to help you make market decisions. Become acquainted with the account executive through phone or personal conversations. His knowledge of the factors entering into the market and understanding of current market trends are important in your final choice.

After making a decision on the brokerage firm and the account executive that would be best for you, contact him and have him send you the literature concerning different contracts and any additional information organization. He will then send you the necessary signature cards required by the firm to open an account and ask you for a deposit of margin money.

You will be trading in regulated commodities, and margin money will be deposited in a segregated fund at the brokerage firm's bank. A segregated account means that the money will only be used for margin and not for expenses of the brokerage firm.

Now you decide to enter into your first trade. Your account executive and you decide to enter into a December Live Cattle contract on the Chicago Mercantile Exchange. Your order will be executed as follows: Your account executive will place this order with the order desk, who will then transmit the order to the floor of the Chicago Mercantile Exchange. There your order will be executed on the trading floor, in the pit. All technical details connected with the transaction will be handled by the brokerage firm.

Upon filling of your order, the filled order will be transmitted back to your account executive, who will then contact you, advising you that you have purchased one December Live Cattle contract at a given price. You will also receive a written confirmation on this transaction. You will now show an open position in December Live Cattle on the books of the brokerage firm.

3

The Mechanics
of Trading

MECHANICS OF A TRADE

Let us go back one step to explain in detail just how your order to buy one December Cattle was handled on the floor of the exchange. All buying and selling in the pit are done by open outcry, and every price change is reported on the exchange ticker system. Each firm has brokers in the different pits, a pit meaning a trading area for the purpose of buying and selling contracts.

When your order was received on the exchange floor, it was time-stamped and then given to a runner. This is a person who takes the order from the desk on the exchange floor and gives it to one of the brokers in the December Cattle trading pit. This broker is then responsible to the brokerage firm to fill that order, if possible, at the stated price. After filling the order, he then has the runner return it to the desk, where it is time-stamped and transmitted back to the order desk at the brokerage house, and the filled order is reported to you.

MARGIN REQUIREMENTS

Futures trading requires you, the trader, to place margin with your brokerage firm. Initial margin is required and this amount varies with each commodity. The minimum margin is established by each commodity exchange. Additional funds are needed when the equity of your account falls below this level. This is known as a maintenance margin call.

All margin calls must be met immediately. Normally you will be given a reasonable amount of time to comply with this request. If you do not comply, the firm has the right to liquidate your trades or a a sufficient number of trades to restore your account to margin requirements.

The brokerage firm has the right to raise margin requirements to the customer at any time. This is normally done if the price of the commodity is changing sharply or if it is the brokerage firm's opinion that due to the volatility of the market the margin requirement is not sufficient at that particular time.

Most commodity contracts have a minimum fluctuation and also a maximum fluctuation for any one particular day. For example, if you are trading Pork Bellies on the Chicago Mercantile Exchange, the fluctuation is considered in points. A point equals $3.80. This means that if you buy a contract at 52.40 and the next price tick is 52.45, you have made a paper profit of 5 points, or $19. The maximum fluctuation on a belly contract is 200 points, so your profit or loss cannot exceed in one day more than 200 points from the previous day's settlement. There are exceptions in some commodity contracts, where the spot month has no limit.

Let us assume that you had originally placed in the hands of your brokerage firm $2,000 margin money and that you and your account executive decide to purchase a December Live Cattle contract whose initial margin is $1,200 with maintenance of $900. After the purchase of the contract your account would show initial margin required $1,299, with excess funds of $800. At the end of each day the settlement price of December Cattle would be applied to your purchase price and your account would be adjusted to either an increase due to profit or decrease due to loss in your contract.

Further, assume that in a period or two or three days there is a decline in the price of the December Cattle contract and your account now shows a loss of $300. Since maintenance margin is only $900 on this contract, you will show an excess of $800 over and above maintenance margin. But in the next four days suppose there is an additional loss of $900. Your account will now need $100 to maintain the maintenance margin and $400 additional in order to bring your account up to initial margin. Your account executive or someone from the margin department of the brokerage firm will then contact you, stating that you must place additional money with the firm in order to maintain the December Cattle contract.

At this point, you must decide whether you should continue with the contract, feeling that it may be profitable in the next few days, and send the brokerage firm the required $400 to maintain your position, or whether to assume your loss and sell the contract.

Let us assume that you decide to sell your December contract at this point and that the selling price causes a loss of $400. Added to this loss would be the commission of $40, so your total loss on the transaction would be $440. A confirmation and purchase and sales statement will be sent to you, showing the original price paid for the contract, the price for which it was sold, the gross loss of $400 plus the commission of $40, making the total loss $440, and your new ledger balance on deposit with the firm as $1,560.

As shown in our example, commission was charged only when the contract was closed out. A single commission is charged for each round-turn transaction consisting of the creation and liquidation of a single contract.

CONTROLLED DISCRETIONARY AND MANAGED ACCOUNTS

There are two methods of trading your account. The first is the professional approach where you and your account executive decide on each trade with no discretion being given directly to your account executive. This method is called a controlled discretionary or managed account. Under this method, you are giving your account executive authorization to trade your account at his discretion at any time and as many times that he considers that a trade should be made. The Chicago Mercantile Exchange and the Board of Trade have rules governing this type of relationship. The following is an excerpt from the CME rule regarding controlled discretionary and managed accounts.

"No clearing member shall accept or carry an account over which any individual or organization, other than the person in whose name the account is carried, exercises trading authority or control, hereinafter referred to as controlled accounts, unless:

"The account is initiated with a minimum of $5,000,* and maintained at a minimum equity of $3,750,* regardless of lesser applicable margin requirements. In determining equity the accounts or ledger balances and positions in all commodities traded at the clearing member shall be included. Whenever at the close of any business day the equity, calculated with all open positions figured to the settling price, in any such account is below the required minimum, the clearing member shall immediately notify the customer in person, by telephone or telegraph and by written confirmation of such notice mailed directly to the customer, not later than the close of the following business day. Such notice shall advise the customer that unless additional funds are promptly received to restore the customer's controlled account to no less than $5,000,* the clearing member shall liquidate all of the customer's open futures positions at the Exchange.

"In the event the call for additional equity is not met within a reasonable time, the customer's entire open position shall be liquidated. No period of time in excess of five business days shall be considered reasonable unless such longer period is approved in writing by an officer or partner of the clearing member upon good cause shown."

*Minimums can be changed by each exchange, so consult your account executive for the current regulations.

REVIEWING YOUR
CONFIRMATIONS AND STATEMENTS

An important factor in trading is that you must be sure that no errors occur in your account. For every trade made you should receive a confirmation, and for every closeout a profit and loss statement, known as a purchase and sale, showing the financial results of each transaction closed out in your account. In addition, a monthly statement showing your ledger balance, your open position, the net profit or loss in all contracts liquidated since the date of your last previous statement, and the net unrealized profit and loss on all open contracts figured to the market should be sent to you.

You should carefully review these statements. Upon receiving a confirmation of a trade you should immediately check its accuracy as far as type of commodity, month, trading price, and quantity of contracts. If this does not agree with your original order, it should be immediately reported to the main office of your brokerage firm, and any differences should be explained and adjustments should be made.

If you do not receive a confirmation on a trade after it was orally reported to you by your account executive, be sure to contact him and the main office so that if an error was made it can be corrected immediately. You should receive written confirmation when you deposit money with your brokerage firm. If within a few days you have not received this confirmation, report it immediately to the main office of your brokerage firm.

Never assume that an order has been filled until you receive an oral confirmation from your broker. A ticker or a board that you may be observing can be running several minutes behind and is not the determining factor as to whether your trade was executed or not. Until you receive this oral confirmation, never reenter an order to buy or sell, against that position.

If you receive a confirmation in the mail showing a trade not belonging to you, immediately notify the main office of your brokerage firm and have them explain why this is on a confirmation with your account number. If it is an error, be sure that it is adjusted immediately and a written confirmation sent to you showing the adjustment of the error. If an error is made and it is profitable to you, do not consider this any differently than if it was not profitable. Regardless of whether there is a profit or loss, all errors should be immediately reported to the brokerage firm.

When you request funds to be mailed from your account, be sure that they are received within a few days from the time of your request. If not, contact the accounting department of the brokerage firm to see what is the cause of the delay.

Never make a check out to an individual. Always make your check out to the brokerage firm.

DAY TRADING

Day trading is where there is a buy and sell made during the trading hours on one particular day. Day trading is not considered to be a sound practice for the new speculator and inexperienced trader. Day trading is something that should be executed only by a sophisticated trader who is in frequent communication with the floor, and even then, on a limited basis.

ORDERS

In order to trade effectively in the commodity market, there are several basic types of orders. The most common order is a market order. A market order is one that you authorize your account executive to buy or sell at the existing price. This is definitely not a predetermined price, but is executed at a bid or offer at that particular moment.
Example: "Buy 5 Feb Pork Bellies at the market."

Limited or Price Orders and "OB" Designation

This type of order to buy or sell commodities at a fixed or "limited" price and the ordinary "market" order are the most common types of orders.

Example: "Buy Three Jan Silver 463.10." This limit order instructs the floor broker to buy three contracts of January Silver futures at 463.10. Even with this simple order, however, one presumption is necessary—that the market price prevailing when the order enters the pit is 463.10 or higher. If the price is below 463.10, the broker could challenge on the basis that the client may have meant "Buy Three Jan Silver 463.10 stop." Therefore, while it is always assumed that a "limit: order means 'or better,'" if possible, it saves confusion and challenges if the "OB" designation is added to the limit price. This is particularly true on orders near the market, or on preopening orders with the limit price based on the previous close, because no one knows whether the opening will be higher or lower than the close, i.e., "Buy Three Jan Silver 463.10 OB."

Stop Orders (Orders Having the Effect of Market Orders)

Buy Stop
Buy stop orders must be written at a price higher than the price prevailing at the time of entry. If the prevailing price for December

Wheat is 456 per bushel, a buy stop order must designate a price above 456.

Example: "Buy 20 Dec Wheat 456½ Day Stop." The effect of this order is that if December Wheat touches 456½, the order to buy 20 December Wheat becomes a market order. From that point, 456½, on, all the above discussion regarding market orders applies.

Sell Stop

Sell stop orders must be written at a price lower than the price prevailing at the time of entry in the trading pit. If the prevailing price of December Wheat is 456 per bushel, a sell stop order must designate a price below 456.

Example: "Sell 20 Dec Wheat 455 Day Stop." If this order enters the trading pit with the above price of 456 prevailing, the order to sell 20 December Wheat becomes a market order. From that point, 455, on, all the above discussion regarding market orders applies.

Buy stop orders have several specific uses. If you are short a December Wheat at 456 and wish to limit your loss to ½ cent per bushel, the above buy stop order at 456½ would serve this purpose. However, it is important to realize that such "stop loss" orders do not actually limit the loss to exactly ½ cent when "elected" or "touched off" because they become market orders and must be executed at whatever price the market conditions dictate.

Another use is when you are without a position and believe that, because of chart analysis or for other reasons, a buy of December Wheat at 456½ would signal the beginning of an important uptrend in wheat prices. Thus, the same order to "Buy 20 Dec Wheat 456½ Day Stop" would serve this purpose.

Sell stop orders have the same uses in reverse. That is, if you are long 20 December Wheat at 456 and wish to limit this loss to 1 cent per bushel, the above sell stop order at 455 would serve this purpose, within the limitations of the market order possibilities. Similarly, if you are without a position and believe that a sale of December Wheat at 455 would signal a downtrend in wheat prices, and you wish to be short the market, you could use the order to "Sell 20 Dec Wheat 455 Day Stop" for this purpose.

Stop Limit Orders
(Variations of Stop Orders)

Stop limit orders should be used by you when you wish to give the floor broker a limit beyond which he cannot go in executing the order that results when a stop price is "elected."

This instructs the broker that when the price of 456½ is reached and "elects" this stop order, instead of making it a market order, it becomes a limited order to be executed at 456½ (or lower), but no higher than 456½.

Example: "Buy one Feb Pork Belly 58.10 Day Stop Limit 58.25" (or any other price above 58.10). This instructs the broker that when the price of 58.10 "elects" the stop order, instead of making it a market order, it becomes a limited order to buy at 58.25 (or lower), but no higher, as with any limit order.

Stop limit orders are particularly useful to you when you have no position and wish to enter a market via the stop order, but want to put some reasonable limit as to what you will pay. On the other hand, stop limit orders are not useful to you when you have an open position and wish to prevent a loss beyond a certain point. The reason is that by limiting the broker to a certain price after a "stop loss" order is elected, *you also run the risk that the market may exceed the limit too fast for the broker to execute.* This would leave you with your original position because the broker would have to wait for the return to the limit before executing. With a straight stop (no limit) order, the broker executes "at the market."

Example: "Buy One Feb Pork Belly 58.10 Day Stop Limit 58.25." Suppose the market moves to 58.10 but then only 20 February Pork Bellies are offered at that price. Your broker in the pit catches the seller's eye first and buys 20 and your broker misses the sale. Your broker then bids 58.20, but the best offer is 58.30. He bids 58.25, but the offer at 58.30 remains unchanged. Then another broker bids for and buys February Pork Bellies at 58.30 and the market moves on up. Your broker is left with no execution to your order unless the market later declines to your limit making a fill possible.

If you did not have a position you might be disappointed, but you would be unhurt financially. However, if you had a position and were trying to limit your loss, you would have defeated your purpose with the stop limit order if you truly wanted "out" after the stop was elected.

Stop limit orders on the sell side have exactly the same uses, advantages, and disadvantages as discussed above, but in reverse:

Example: "Sell 20 Dec Wheat 455 Day Stop Limit." This means that when the market declines to 455 per bushel, the broker may sell at 455 (or higher), but no lower.

Another example: "Sell One Feb Pork Belly 58.25 Stop Limit 58.10." This instructs the broker to sell a belly after the stop price of 58.25 is reached and "elects" the stop order, but no lower than 58.10.

MIT Orders
(Market-If-Touched)

By adding MIT (market-if-touched) to a limit order, the limit order will have the effect of a market order when the limit price is reached or touched. This type of order is useful to you when you have an open position and if a certain limit price is reached.

Example: "Sell One Sept Sugar 950 MIT." The floor broker is told that if and when the price of September Sugar rises to 9½ cents per pound, he is to sell one contract at the market. At this price of 9½ cents all prior discussion on market orders applies.

Under certain market conditions, not enough contracts are bid at 9½ cents to fill all offers to sell. Thus, you may see your straight limit price appear on the ticker, but your broker fails to make the sale.

But by adding MIT to the limit price, you will receive an execution, because the order becomes a market order if the price is touched. However, the price will not necessarily be a good one in your eyes, since it became a market order when touched.

The same reasoning is true on the buy side of MIT orders, but in reverse. Assume you are short one contract of September Sugar, with the prevailing price at 9½ cents per pound and you want to cover or liquidate your short at 9 cents.

Example: "Buy One Sept Sugar 9¢ MIT." If and when the price of September Sugar declines to 9 cents per pound, the floor broker must buy one contract at the market. Aside from the disadvantages of any market order, the MIT designation on the buy order prevents the disappointment that might arise if a straight limit buy at 9 cents were entered without the MIT added.

Spread Orders

Spread is a simultaneous long or short position in the same or related commodity. Thus, a spread order would be to buy one month of a certain commodity and sell another month of the same commodity, or buy one month of one commodity and sell the same or another month of a related commodity.

Example: "Buy 5 July Beans Market and Sell 5 May Beans Market" or "Buy 10 Kansas City Dec Wheat Market and Sell 10 Chicago May Wheat Market."

Another example: "Buy 5 May Corn Market and Sell 5 May Wheat Market."

In the example of the related commodity spread, normally the reason you would use such a spread is that you expect to make a profit out of an expected tightness in the Corn Market, in the hope the corn contract will gain in value faster than wheat.

There may be a situation where you have a position either long or short in the commodity and want to change to a nearer or more distant option of the same commodity. For example, you are long 5,000 bushels of May Soybeans on May 20 and want to avoid a delivery notice by moving your position forward into the July option. The basic spread order would be:

"Buy 5 July Beans Market and Sell 5 May Beans Market."

Sometimes you may prefer not to use market orders, in which case you use the difference spread.

Example: "Buy 5 July Beans and Sell 5 May Beans July 2¢ Over." Even though the prices of the two options are not specified, the broker is allowed to execute at any time he can do so with July selling at 2 cents or less above May. Over or under designations are a necessity for clarity to the floor broker. Omitting either is like omitting the price.

All orders, except market orders, can be canceled prior to execution. Naturally, a market order is executed immediately upon reaching the pit, so its cancellation is almost impossible.

4

Additional Trading Techniques

Two additional trading techniques are the switch (also referred to as the spread or straddle) and the cash and carry.

SWITCH (SPREAD/STRADDLE)

1. Look at nearby months:

   December Gold   *April Gold*
   396   415.80

   Assumption: Inflation will continue to make gold a desirable investment.

2. Decide to buy April and sell December.
3. Tell broker to "buy switch" at $19.80 (415.80 − 396) (switch requires ½ margin because of off setting positions).
4. Hold position 3–4 weeks, then look at contract months, tell broker to "unwind switch":

December Gold	*April Gold*
Buy 1 contract @ 446	Sell 1 contract @ 475.80
396	415.80
Loss on Dec. + (50)	Gain on April + 60

   Net Gain = $10/03. × 100 03. = $1,000.

CASH AND CARRY

Dec. '80 = 703

June '81 = 758

Purchase 100 oz. gold @ $703 in cash market sell 1 contract gold on Comex to mature 6/81 @ 758.

Premium over Cash Market

$$\frac{55}{703} \quad \times \quad \frac{360}{180} \quad \times \quad \frac{100}{1} = 15\%$$

Borrow the $70M at 14% (fixed rate)

Around 6/81 deliver 100 oz. to close out the Comex contract.

Profit = $75,800 − ($70,300 + $4,921 int. cost) = $579.

In summary, here are some rules for successful trading:

1. *Go with the trend.* Go with prices when they leave a congestion. When Wheat, Beans, Corn, and Soybean Meal make new season highs, the trader should go along regardless of his feelings. The pit prices are the supreme judge of who is right and who is wrong. The markets are not straight one-way—there are reactions. If you desire, buy half of your commitment on new highs and the other half on the reaction. But remember, the reaction may not come for some time.
2. If after making a new season high the markets close lower on volume, *get out and watch*, as it indicates a danger sign. If it closes on the bottom and opens with a down gap the next day, *absolutely get out and wait or go short against the high or gap.* The reverse is true on season lows.
3. Always trade with stops. The first loss is the cheapest loss. The place to pray is church, not in the pits. If you are stopped out and the market reverses, go with it again.
4. *Let your profits ride, moving your stops with the market. NEVER* decide on your profit when the market breaks out of its range. This does not apply when it trades within a range.
5. *Buy the strongest option of the commodity.* If you want to spread, sell the weakest.
6. *Never let a profit turn into a loss.*
7. *Don't overtrade* or you will be whipsawed to death in a turbulent market as prices go forth to and from until the proper level is found.
8. *If you don't know, stay out!* The best traders are those who don't trade every tick.
9. If you're wrong, one contract is too many. If you're right, one contract is not enough within your prudent margin requirements.
10. If the market closes on new season highs or new season highs close on the limit up, *be long* that contract. The reverse is true.
11. If all the other markets close lower on the bottom and one commodity closes higher, be long that contract. The reverse is true.
12. If one contract closes limit up, and finally at the end of the day one of the other contracts comes limit up, be short the contract that closes limit up last.

13. Have self-control; don't go overboard.
14. Be even on the eve of a government report and then go with the market.
15. Be respectful of gaps. Most are closed, but the unclosed few are strong trend indicators.

II

SPECULATING
IN FINANCIAL FUTURES

5

The Use of Technical
Analysis to Derive
a Price Forecast

Technical analysis deals exclusively with market activity to develop a price forecast. As an investor, you are looking for a way to make a prediction about the future price of a commodity. Technical analysts look at prices, trading volume, and open interest to determine price forecasts.

The oldest method of technical market analysis has to do with interpreting the patterns of investment on price charts. The two most common charts are "bar" and "point and figure." Bar charts illustrate the range and close of prices during a fixed time period (weekly). Point and figure charts use a figured amount of price change to illustrate forward and backward pattern investments.

A typical bar chart is shown in Figure 1, page 26.

Figure 1 shows a clear downtrend in the June 1982 gold contract traded on the Comex in New York. Gold trading has enjoyed tremendous growth since it began in the United States in 1975. From January to December of 1981, 10.3 million contracts have traded on the Comex. This compares to 8 million for all of 1980, 6.5 million for 1979, 3.7 million for 1978, 1 million in 1977, and .5 million in 1976. The bull market in gold began in the early 1970s with prices at about $25 per ounce. As world inflation accelerated, gold moved to $200 per ounce by December 1974. At this point, gold became available to Americans, but instead of the instant bull market many people anticipated, prices fell to $100 by mid-1976. Then the real move began. Gold reached $875 in early 1980 but collapsed soon after. By the end of March 1980, the nearest gold future fell to $450, another 50 percent decline. This one occurred in less than three months. Then we saw a rally above $700 for the nearby contract, and the present decline began. The bear move coincided with falling prices of other commodities and with a general

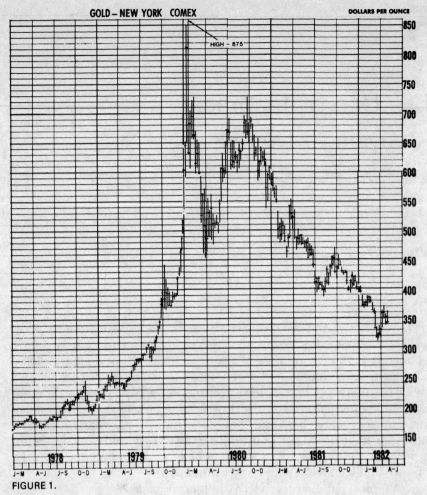

HIGH – 875

850

800

750

700

650

600

550

500

450

400

350

300

250

200

150

1978   1979   1980   1981   1982

J–M   A–J   J–S   O–D   J–M   A–J   J–S   O–D   J–M   A–J   J–S   O–D   J–M   A–J   J–S   O–D   J–M   A–J

FIGURE 1.

decline in inflation rates. The $400 level has twice provided good support for gold. However, any penetration of the $400 support level would signal new lows for the contract.

The reader is referred to *Technical Analysis of Stock Trends,* by Robert D. Edwards and John Magee (Springfield, Mass.: John Magee Inc., 1948), and to *Commodity Trading Systems and Methods,* by Perry Kaufman (New York: Wiley, 1979), for a further discussion of technical analysis. The reader should also remember that "open interest" refers to the number of open "contracts." It refers to unliquidated purchases or sales and never to their combined total. You are concerned with open interest because the greater the number of contracts outstanding, the easier it will be for you to liquidate a position without seriously depressing the price of the contract. High volume and open interest levels suggest that increasing volatility will be experienced in the markets. This calls for even greater diversification and proper money management techniques on the part of the investor.

6

Interest-Rate Futures

This chapter will develop the concept of interest-rate futures. In subsequent chapters we will deal with currency futures.

To begin with, what are interest-rate futures?

Interest-rate futures are contracts or agreements to make or take delivery of a specified amount of a certain financial instrument (GNMAs, commercial paper, U.S. treasury bills, bonds, or notes) at a specific future date at a price established at the time of the contract.

The financial technique that companies use to manage the risk of fluctuating interest rates is called hedging. For example, a pension fund manager who will have $1 million to invest in three months and is concerned that yields may fall from their current levels can use the futures market for protection. The financial manager can take action now in the futures market that anticipates what he intends to do later when the money is contributed to the pension fund. His purpose is to ensure today the yield/price combination that may not exist on that future day. While the prices of futures contracts and the underlying actual security do not move in lockstep, they do move together, creating a market in which interest risks can be offset. If he cannot purchase treasury bonds now because he does not have the money, he can buy a treasury bond futures contract with an equivalent yield. If yields fall, it will cost him more in three months to purchase the actual treasury bonds, but his futures contract will have risen a commensurate amount. This means he can determine the yield in advance, which, of course, means better money management.

Who uses interest-rate futures? Professional money managers who wish to shift the risk of fluctuating interest rates such as pension fund managers.

The uncertain cost of money these days and the fluctuating yield on investment make strategic planning with specific objectives more important now than ever before. The purpose of hedging interest rates is to protect the hedger against major adverse moves. In this regard, interest-rate futures offer a risk management tool to those exposed to potential losses related to changing interest rates.

Various applications of interest-rate futures are useful methods of reducing uncertainty and avoiding risks. Futures can be used to pre-determine the desired levels of interest both from a revenue and from an expense point of view. The key question is the effect of not taking advantage of the benefits of interest-rate futures.

Why should I buy treasury bonds, for example, instead of sell them if I think interest rates are going down? Let's look at a treasury bond example. The futures contract in U.S. treasury bonds is a basic trading unit of $100,000 having a fixed interest rate of 8 percent. When the treasury bond yield is 8 percent, the bond will trade at 100. If interest rates decline from 8 to 7½ percent, the price would increase to reflect the prevailing yield in the treasury bond market. The same is true for treasury bills. The futures price quotation is the difference between the annual yield and 100. Thus, if treasury bills are yielding 9 percent on an annual basis, the quote would be 91. If interest rates fall to 8 percent, the price of the T-bill contract would rise to 92. If interest rates rise, the converse would be true and prices would decline.

Isn't all this really speculating? No for hedgers, yes for specu-lators. The speculator assumes the risk or price change that the hedger seems to avoid. The speculator does so in exchange for the opportunity to profit. When the speculator assumes the price risk, he allows the hedger to concentrate on the more controllable aspects of his business. Futures speculation is unlike most investments in that price move-ments are magnified by the extremely high leverage allowed by deposit requirements, which represent a small portion of the full value of the contract. To purchase a futures contract in treasury bonds having a $100,000 market value requires an initial deposit (at this writing) of $2,250. To purchase a futures contract of $1 million in treasury bills, the initial requirement is (at this writing) $1,700. While leverage can mean additional margin deposits depending on market fluctuations, the hedger's physical position should be offset by a comparable futures position.

Example:

Investor Smith bought (went "long") a contract at 68.00. Investor Jones sold a contract (went "short") at the same price. Each put up initial margin of $3,500. The settlement price at the end of the day was 68.75, an increase of 15 ticks (75/5 = 15) having a value of $375 (15 x $25 = $375). That amount is credited to Investor Smith's "long" account. The same amount is debited to Investor Jones' "short" account:

Account After One Day	Smith (Long)	Jones (Short)
Initial Margin (Original Equity)	$3,500	$3,500
Daily Mark to Market	375	(375)
Current Equity	$3,875	$3,125

After Several Weeks

At the end of several weeks, the futures contract has appreciated to 72.05. The aggregate change in market value since Smith and Jones bought and sold their contracts is + $2,025.

Current Value	72.05
Initial Value	68.00
Change in Value	4.05 x $500 = $2,025

Investor Smith's account is credited with an aggregate profit of $2,025, which he can withdraw, if he wishes. Investor Jones' loss of the same amount has brought his equity below the required maintenance level of $1,500, and he receives a margin call for funds to bring the account back up to $3,500.

Account	Smith (Long)	Jones (Short)
Initial Margin (Original Equity)	$3,500	$3,500
Cumulative Mark to Market	2,025	(2,025)
Current Equity	$5,525	$1,475
Withdrawable Excess	$2,025	
Margin Call		$2,025

FIGURE 2. Brokerage Statement of Financial Futures

7

Treasury Bills
Futures Trading

TREASURY BILLS

Treasury bills, direct obligations of the U. S. Treasury, constitute by far the largest segment of the money markets, both in the volume of new issues sold by the Treasury and in secondary-market trading volume. Banks, corporations, foreign governments, and individuals purchase 3-month (13-week) T-bills because they are the nearest thing to cash and are also an earning asset.

The Fed, acting as an agent for the Treasury, sells 3-month (13-week) and 6-month (182-day) T-bills through a weekly auction held on Monday afternoon. Competitive bids are accepted from Thursday until 1:30 P.M., New York time, Monday, although most bids are submitted just prior to the deadline because of the volatility of T-bill rates. T-bills are sold on a discount basis—less than their face value—and are redeemed at par on maturity. The dollar difference between the discount price and face value is the interest earned on a T-bill investment. Settlement is made each Thursday with the buyer making payment to the Fed in either mature T-bills or federal funds, which are basically reserves of members' banks that can be used for short-term transactions. The so-called 90-day (or 13-week) T-bill generally matures ninety-one days from the date of issue, but may mature ninety or ninety-two days from issue because of holidays.

Primary Market

The Treasury sells T-bills primarily to finance the federal government's short-term cash needs, including refunding of maturing T-bills. The size of each issue is determined by the Treasury Department and is dependent on several factors: the amount of maturing T-bills to be refunded, the near-term cash needs of the Treasury, the level of interest rates, and the Fed's monetary-policy objectives. The effective yield on new issues depends on the level of bids received and accepted by the Fed and is closely related to current and anticipated rates for other money market instruments. About two thirds of each new issue is bought by the major banks and government securities dealers; the remainder goes to corporations, state and local governments, foreign central banks, and individuals. These purchasers buy 3-month (13-week) T-bills to convert excess cash into a low-risk, high-liquidity, interest-earning asset.

Rates on treasury bills exhibit a seasonal pattern, since the Treasury typically does the bulk of its financing in the latter half of the year. Bills maturing after year end also may be popular with those who want no further income in the current tax year. In the spring of each year, bill prices typically rise (interest rate declines) as tax collections increase and the Treasury pays down (lowers) its debt.

Secondary Market

The cash or secondary market for T-bills is maintained by nearly three dozen primary dealers approved by the Federal Reserve Board. The most important role of these bank and nonbank dealers is to make ready markets for T-bills and other government securities. The dealers act as speculators for their own accounts by taking long or short positions in the markets; they can buy securities into their inventories or sell to customers (smaller banks, corporations, and other institutional buyers).

Dealer spreads are typically 2 to 4 basis points ($50 to $100 per $1 million); no commissions are charged to margins required, since all transactions are for cash.

Volatility

Yields on T-bills can fluctuate rapidly as money market conditions change. Factors influencing yields include "tone" of the market (i.e., activity and aggressiveness of dealers), rates on other money market instruments, Federal Open Market Committee (FOMC) trading activity, and other considerations (such as long-term yields and inflation rates).

Weekly price volatility in recent years at times approached $5,000 per $1 million and has averaged about $500 per $1 million (which would be 20 basis points on an IMM futures contract). The movement of yields on 3-month (13-week) T-bills over that period included swings of as much as 183 basis points in a week's time.

SOME ECONOMIC INDICATORS

What makes interest rates fluctuate from day to day? What economic factors can affect the money market? Will increased inflation rates be bullish or bearish for the market?

These questions and many more are of great importance to anyone dealing in interest-rate-sensitive instruments. The fundamental factors affecting interest rates are neither independent nor static—the net effect of these factors is constantly changing.

Money is much like any other commodity and is therefore subject to the laws of supply and demand. In financial markets supply and demand are brought into balance or equilibrium by the price of funds, which is the rate of interest. The investor or supplier seeks the highest rate of return possible while the borrower, or demand element, seeks to borrow at the lowest rate of interest. Many banks, corporations, individuals, and the Federal Reserve are involved in seeking or supplying funds (sometimes doing both simultaneously when advantageous) in the money market.

There are many economic factors affecting treasury bill prices and money market interest rates. Among the most important are (1) Federal Reserve activity, (2) technical "tone" of the money market, (3) financial needs of the business community, and (4) condition of the economy.

The Federal Reserve

By far the most important determinant of T-bill rates is the Federal Reserve System. The actions most frequently implemented include (1) trading government securities through FOMC operations to dealers, thus increasing or decreasing bank reserves; (2) changing reserve requirements, thus altering levels of loanable funds; and (3) adjusting the discount rate (the Fed's lending rate to banks). In addition, the Fed will auction greater or lesser amounts of T-bills, again to increase or decrease bank reserves and thereby control the amount of loanable funds. Federal policy on matters such as inflation, growth of the money supply, or funding Treasury deficits can precipitate these actions. Such activities influence expectations and responses among financial market participants and can set into motion a chain reaction across the whole spectrum of interest rates.

Open Market Operation

The Federal Open Market Committee is the Fed's most important policymaking body, having responsibility for Fed buying and selling of government securities. This trading influences interest rates and the availability of credit. When the Fed buys securities from a commercial bank, it pays in short-term Fed funds credited to the reserve account of the selling bank. This results in an increase of loanable funds and a decrease in interest rates. When the Fed sells securities, the buyer's reserve account is debited. This results in a reduction of credit and a firming of interest rates.

On a day-to-day basis the Fed relies exclusively on its System Open Market Account, which is maintained by the FOMC. Treasury bills, in terms of both dollar value and influence on other interest rates, are the most important money market instrument used by the FOMC in the Fed's daily operations. In 1974, for example, gross purchases by the FOMC amounted to $13.5 billion; T-bills accounted for 85 percent of the total, or $11.7 billion. The FOMC's gross sales in 1974 totaled $5.8 billion, virtually all in T-bills.

Bank Reserve Requirements

The Fed's tool with the most far-reaching monetary impact is the control over member-bank reserve requirements. Changes in the required level of bank reserves determine the amount of bank monetary expansion. If reserves required against existing deposits are lowered, there is generally an expansion in bank credit and in the funds available for lending. If reserve requirements are raised, bank credit and the amount of funds available for lending generally contract. Changes in reserve requirements can drastically shift the amount of loans that the reserves will allow.

The Fed can raise or lower reserve requirements within limits, varying from 10 to 22 percent for Reserve-city banks and 7 to 14 percent for banks not located in Federal Reserve cities.

The Discount Rate

Borrowing from the Federal Reserve is usually accomplished by banks using their own (promissory) notes, which are secured by government securities. Changes in the discount rate are often regarded as indicating fundamental shifts in the Fed credit policy. Such shifts are immediately reflected by the financial market, sometimes even anticipated by it.

Changes in the discount rate have an immediate effect on the Fed's member banks. There is a virtual chain reaction through the financial markets. When the discount rate is increased, banks are generally inclined to sell government securities, especially treasury bills, rather than expand borrowings at the Federal Reserve discount window; the sale of securities reduces securities prices while raising their yields, higher yields in the T-bill market finally spreading to other money market instruments and into the capital market. Should the discount rate be lowered, Fed discount borrowing is likely to be increased, thereby stimulating the commercial banks to hold greater amounts of government securities.

Tone

The activity and aggressiveness of dealers in government securities can affect the direction and volatility of all interest rates. This is known as market tone. The market's interpretation of the Fed's actions, the nation's economic well-being, and social and political events have a major influence on trading. The tone is also sensitive to governmental monetary policy, fiscal policy, debt management, and international policy, particularly if a change in any of these areas signals a turning point in interest-rate movements. The technical analyst believes that price, volume, and pace are reflective of all the market participants' opinions. This emphasis on market activity rather than on the causes of such activity can affect the tone of trading. On the other hand, the psychology of the market may run counter to technical information; expectation and anticipation are important elements of market tone.

Business Cash Demand

Industry's demand for cash has a strong influence on short-term interest-rate movements. Increased bank borrowings create more demand deposits in the commercial banking system, which, in turn, increase the money supply. The demand for loans increases and rates rise on bank loans, commercial paper, and other sources of short-term financing. On the other hand, loan demand may decrease because of such circumstances as inventory liquidation or lagging industrial production. This would exert downward pressure on interest rates. Indicators of short-term business-loan demand include new orders in durable-goods industries, contracts and orders on plants and equipment, change in book value of inventories, industrial production, and levels of commercial and industrial loans outstanding.

Economic Conditions

Another significant indicator of interest-rate direction and volatility is the condition of the economy. A stable economic situation will help create a stable money market, whereas a period of economic uncertainty could lead to wide interest-rate fluctuation. Such measures of the economic condition as gross national product, balance of trade levels, unemployment, inflation, and housing starts help determine the relative strength or weakness of the economy. Data on these and other figures are released at various intervals and can have great impact on interest rates depending on how essential they are to the economic outlook. In addition, newspapers and business journals regularly provide information on and evaluation of all aspects of the condition of the economy. The sources of economic comment may be official or unofficial; nevertheless, they bear watching and must be analyzed in light of all current circumstances.

HOW HEDGING CAN AID
FINANCIAL MANAGERS

Any commitment in the money markets exposes both borrowers and lenders to the risk of interest-rate changes for as long as the debt instrument is outstanding. Hedging is the action taken to protect business or assets against an unforeseen change in price or value. Applied to T-bills, it is a vehicle used by lenders or borrowers of money market funds when they buy or sell a futures contract(s) as a temporary substitute for an actual lending or borrowing transaction to be made at a later date. Hedgers know they will be participating as borrowers or lenders in the "cash" or "immediate" market at some specific time. They use the futures market to provide forward price protection for their anticipated money market transactions.

Who Can Hedge
Interest-Rate Risk?

Any institution that has a significant portion of its assets and/or liabilities committed to interest-rate-sensitive vehicles can use a futures market to hedge this exposure. In addition to considering the proportion of rate-sensitive exposure, financial managers should also consider the impact of interest income or expense on their organizations' earnings; for many companies, interest rates alone have caused big earnings declines or increases.

Potential hedgers in interest-rate futures include banks, corporations, nonbank financial institutions, government securities dealers, trust departments, mutual funds, pension funds, real estate investment trusts, and finance companies. Any financial manager with present or planned commitments in treasury bills, federal agency paper, commercial paper, certificates of deposit, bankers' acceptances, bank loans tied to prime, or floating-rate notes should seriously consider using the futures markets to hedge his exposure to interest-rate fluctuation.

Hedging Interest-Rate
Exposure with T-Bills

A treasury bill futures contract can be used by a hedger to provide interest-rate protection on other money market instruments, such as commercial paper. The effectiveness of the hedge will be determined by the extent to which movements in the rates for T-bills parallel the movement in rates for the other instrument. For example, if a perfect correlation existed between movements in T-bills and commercial paper, then a T-bill futures contract would be a very efficient device for hedging changes in commercial paper rates. The closer the compatibility, the more nearly perfect the hedge.

HEDGING AND CORRELATION

Correlation is the degree to which yields or price fluctuations of one money market instrument are simultaneously matched by those of another such instrument. When the correlation is high, one can do a very efficient job of hedging, since yield or price fluctuation in the one market will be closely matched in the other market.

Even in instances in which the correlation is not perfect and is unstable, an imperfect hedge can be much better than no hedge at all. For example, if commercial paper normally trades at a +25 to +150-point range over T-bills, one might think that a T-bill futures would be a poor hedge mechanism for commercial paper rates. However, if the volatility of T-bills and commercial paper is such that a 300-point change in absolute rates is highly probable, then even a 150-point exposure is preferable to the 300-point exposure of the nonhedged position.

Since the T-bill market is the principal center from which interest-rate movements emanate, a T-bill futures contract can be an efficient vehicle for hedging interest-rate movements in other money instruments. To determine the efficiency and value of the hedge, one must simply compare the volatility of the correlative relationships to the relative volatility of the absolute rates for each instrument.

A study made prior to the opening of T-bill futures trading revealed a high statistical correlation between selected money market instruments and T-bills—evidence of the effectiveness of T-bill futures for hedging interest-rate risk arising from other money instruments. For example, the correlation coefficient between 13-week T-bills versus 13-week prime bankers' acceptances was .883, versus 13-week prime commercial paper .855, and versus 13-week certificates of deposit .854. The study was based on weekly data 1973 through June 1975.

The average weekly price changes among money market instruments were quite similar, 1973 through July 1977. The average weekly price change for 13-week treasury bills was 17 basis points, for certificates of deposit 17 basis points, for 90-119-day prime commercial paper 15 basis points, for 90-day bankers' acceptances 13 basis points, and for federal funds 18 basis points.

POTENTIAL USERS
OF T-BILL FUTURES

As mentioned earlier, both borrowers and investors (lenders) are exposed to the risk of interest-rate changes whenever they make a commitment in the money markets. Following is a sampling of institutions that might use the T-bill futures market to hedge this risk when they are committed in the money markets or anticipate entering such markets at some future time:

1. Corporate Treasurers
   A. Long hedge. Buy T-bill futures as a hedge against interest-rate decline on future money market investments.
   B. Short hedge. Sell T-bill futures as a hedge against increasing interest-rate costs on future short-term bank borrowings.
2. Banks
   A. Long hedge. Buy futures to protect the government securities trading area against falling interest rates on future purchases.
   B. Long hedge. The trust department will be able to hedge the return on the rollover of its short-term money market instruments.
   C. Short hedge. Sell futures to hedge cost of future CD purchases, Euro-dollar borrowings, repos, fed funds.
3. Savings and Loan Associations
   A. Long hedge. Buy T-bill futures contracts to hedge the return on variable-rate loans.
   B. Long hedge. Buy futures during times of falling interest rates to lock in a rollover yield for already owned securities and anticipated investments.
   C. Short hedge. Sell T-bill futures to protect the value of bills in the portfolio against devaluation caused by rising interest rates.
   D. Short hedge. Sell T-bill futures to protect against disintermediation.
4. Municipalities
   A. Long hedge. Buy futures to lock in interest income on proceeds of bond sales or revenues not immediately spent.
   B. Short hedge. Sell futures to lock in cost of anticipated short-term borrowings.

HEDGING AGAINST FALLING INTEREST RATES

A financial manager who anticipates having funds to lend (i.e., invest) in the short-term money markets at a known time in the future can hedge against the risk that rates may drop by the time such funds are actually available. He does this by buying a futures contract now at a specified rate for delivery at a specified future time. If rates go down between the purchase date and the delivery date, the contract will appreciate in value. (This happens because of a basic financial relationship: when interest rates go down, prices on money market instruments go up.) The contract's appreciation in value on the futures contract can be applied to the investor's "opportunity loss" from the actual decline in the "cash" or "spot" money markets. An investor can minimize both downside risk and upside potential through a futures market hedge. For investors anticipating receipt of loanable funds, the appropriate futures market hedge is a "long" or "buy" hedge.

Example of a Long Hedge

Treasury Bill Rollover
   The following hypothetical example shows how a money manager could use the T-bill futures market to establish the yield he will

receive when he reinvests or "rolls over" his portfolio. The same technique would be used to establish in advance a rate on a money market instrument to be purchased at a future time by this same money manager, for example, a corporate treasurer.

Cash Market		Futures Market	
Sept. 15			
Bought $5 million in T-bills @ 9%		Bought 5 Dec. contracts @ 9%	
Cost	$4,886,250	Value	$4,887,500
Dec. 10			
Rolled over $5 million in T-bills @ 7%		Sold (offset) 5 Dec. contracts @ 7%	
Cost	$4,911,528	Value	$4,912,500
LOSS	$ 25,278	PROFIT	$ 25,000

HEDGING AGAINST RISING INTEREST RATES

Borrowers in the money markets also can use interest-rate futures to protect themselves against increases in short-term rates with a "short" or "sell" hedge. A short hedge in the futures market is used to offset increased borrowing costs. The financial manager simply sells now an interest-rate contract for future delivery. If rates rise between the contract sale date and its delivery date, the value of the futures contract will drop and the hedger can make a gain by buying back, for a lower price, the contract he sold previously at a higher price. With the gain from his futures contract, the borrower is able to offset the increase in his cash borrowing costs. Of course, if borrowing rates drop instead of rise, the hedger's lower-than-anticipated cost of borrowing has been offset by a loss on the futures contract. As with the investor's long hedge, the borrower's short hedge has minimized both his downside risk and his upside potential. But during the period prior to making his "spot" transaction, he has had insurance against an adverse interest-rate move, and that is what he wanted.

Example of a Short Hedge

Commercial Paper Hedge
This example shows how a borrower who plans to issue commercial paper could protect himself against higher future interest costs by hedging in the T-bill market.

A borrower who plans in May to sell $10 million in 90-day commercial paper in September can hedge that sale by taking a short position in the futures market.

Cash Market	Futures Market

May 1

Anticipated selling $10 million commercial paper in Sept. (Current rate—5.38%)	Sold 10 Sept. T-bill contracts @ 5.20% Value $9,870,000

September 5

Sold $10 million commercial paper @ 6.63%		Bought (offset) 10 Sept. T-bill contracts @ 6.59%	
Revenue	$9,834,250		
Interest cost	165,750	Value	$9,835,250
Less hedge profit	−34,750	Profit from futures	$ 34,750
	$ 131,000		
EFFECTIVE INTEREST RATE	5.24%		

In this example the actual interest cost is reduced by $34,750 (the profit made on the hedge) to $131,000, and the effective interest rate is reduced to 5.24%. Because Treasury bill yields and commercial-paper rates move in close tandem, T-bill futures can provide protection against adverse interest-rate fluctuation.

DEVELOPING A CORPORATE HEDGING STRATEGY FOR SHORT-TERM INSTRUMENTS

In order to use the treasury bill futures market effectively as a hedging device, there are several questions a financial manager should consider.

1. What is the organization's exposure? In evaluating interest-rate exposure, money market liabilities should be subtracted from money market assets (investments). These liabilities could include bank borrowings tied to the prime rate, commercial paper, certificates of deposit, bankers' acceptances to be issued, or floating-rate note issues. Also included should be the short-term debt of any consolidated subsidiary that may have significant money market exposure.

Net exposure at any point in time may be "long" if there is money to invest, or "short" if there are more rate-sensitive liabilities than assets. For example, if $150 million is invested in money market instruments, and short-term bank borrowings total $50 million, the net exposure is $100 million on the long side. As the $100 million "long" exposure earns interest, that estimated amount should be added to the "long" exposure. It can be helpful at this point to estimate what the effect on cash flow and the income statement might be, using a range of possible interest rates applied to the net exposure.

2. Are there seasonal or cyclical factors in a company's interest-rate exposure? After estimating the company's net annual exposure, seasonal qualities should be considered. A company may have a long exposure during some periods of the year and a short exposure at other times.

This sort of picture could apply to retailers, transportation companies, agribusiness firms, and others. There also may be cyclical influences on an organization's interest-rate exposure. For example, a firm in the building-products industry may have a long exposure during a building boom and a short exposure during a recession.

3. *What is the company's hedgeable base?* After the size and nature of exposure have been analyzed, it becomes necessary to estimate what the exposure will be over the next three months to a year. Rather than try to pinpoint the exact exposure, the financial manager should estimate a range. For example, if estimated exposure is $50 million to $75 million long in the first quarter of the fiscal year, the firm's hedgeable base would be $50 million. If a firm "hedges" more than what its actual exposure will be, then it, in effect, is speculating. This can be risky if the additional exposure doesn't materialize because of changing business conditions. A reliable forecast, therefore, is important.

4. *How much risk should be taken?* Now that the base exposure has been determined, it may be decided that certain risks in the money markets would be wise in order to benefit if rates move advantageously. However, risking full money market exposure might be imprudent. It may be concluded that the company is unwilling to risk paying more than $10 million in interest costs and wants to hedge a portion of its exposure. By doing so, it will hedge or lock in both a maximum borrowing cost and a minimum borrowing cost. The amount of hedging a firm does should depend on its willingness to accept risk. If no hedge position is taken at all, the company is effectively speculating with 100 percent of its interest-rate exposure.

5. *What is the firm's basis?* After it has been decided how much exposure is to be hedged, the composition of that exposure, and the estimated correlation between rates on that exposure and treasury bills, the hedging medium should be studied. For example, if net exposure consists of $50 million in commercial paper, the relationship between T-bill rates and commercial paper rates should be evaluated.

6. *What is the outlook for short-term interest rates?* Hedging strategy should be based in part on an assessment of the direction money market rates might take over the next six months to a year. Whether a company does its own forecasting or relies on the views of economists, bankers, and others, it should compare this assessment with the futures market rates before hedging.

CORPORATE TREASURERS

The treasury bill futures market can provide valuable protection to the corporate treasurer in both his borrowing and investing functions. By carefully assessing his net exposure in interest-rate-sensitive areas, he can devise a hedging strategy that will provide protection whether his position is short or long.

During the time it takes to develop a financial plan to obtain short-term funds and to actually get the loan arranged or the commercial paper placed, significant changes in interest rates can occur. But if the treasurer were to sell contracts in the futures market, he could hedge the interest rate for his future cash borrowing. On the other hand, the corporate cash manager may have sizable cash inflows to invest in short-term marketable securities. Often he must sacrifice yield on his portfolio in order to obtain the security and liquidity dictated by corporate objectives. When hedging in the T-bill futures market, a cash manager can buy a contract at any time when he sees an interest rate at an acceptable level in an acceptable option (delivery) month. Judicious use of the T-bill futures market can help him match interest rates on borrowings and investments. This market can also supply him with a view of market expectations on future interest-rate levels. Such information is valuable in establishing the maturity mix in a portfolio, depending on the market's anticipation of higher or lower short-term interest rates, six, nine, twelve, fifteen, or even eighteen months out.

MONEY FUND MANAGERS

Many money funds, cash management funds, and other mutual funds have expanded in recent years. Their main purpose has been to offer individuals and institutions some participation in short-term money market investments. Funds of this type attempt to maximize income while preserving principal and liquidity.

The manager of a money fund whose cash investments are in various types of money market instruments such as CDs and commercial paper, in addition to T-bills, can effectively use a futures contract in 3-month T-bills. By anticipating the size and approximate dates of investment in these and other money market vehicles, the fund manager can buy the number of contracts necessary to cover some part of his future interest-rate exposure and lock in an acceptable return on at least part of his portfolio. Because the correlations between T-bill rates and yields on other money market instruments are so close, the T-bill futures contract can be used to hedge the return on many different short-term investments. The long hedge can be offset in the futures market at any time and the money market instrument bought in the cash market. If the manager chose to invest in T-bills, he could take delivery on his contract. In either case, he would have established the rate of interest on his investments well in advance of his actual cash transactions. Any profit realized by the decline of interest rates and corresponding increased proceeds from the sale of the contract(s) would offset the lowered interest rates available in the cash market at the future time. On the other hand, if the manager's forecast is wrong and short-term rates increase, with a corresponding dip in prices, the loss realized in the sale of his futures contract will be offset by the gain in the cash market, and he will have had relatively inexpensive risk insurance in the interim.

INSURANCE, TRUST, AND PENSION FUND MANAGERS

Fund managers who act as fiduciaries will find the T-bill futures market a valuable tool with which to guarantee a yield on a short-term security. These organizations keep a portion of their assets in cash and cash equivalents to meet payouts to beneficiaries and to meet general cash needs, such as for buying longer-term bonds or stocks. A stable base-income level on funds in this category can be maintained by buying futures contracts whenever an acceptable rate is offered and locking in that rate of return on at least a portion of the anticipated cash investments. This protection is maintained by offsetting a position before delivery becomes necessary and establishing a new position in a later contract month. By "rolling over" the position at acceptably high interest rates, the manager can minimize his exposure to falling interest rates in the cash market.

PORTFOLIO MANAGERS

The T-bill futures market can add significantly to efficient capital management by banks and other financial institutions that have a large percentage of their commitments in long-term fixed-interest-rate instruments. Many bond portfolios contain older bonds carrying relatively low interest-rate returns. By taking advantage of a short-term interest-rate futures market and taking either a long or short position on anticipated short-term interest-rate changes, an institution can realize gains that will upgrade total investment returns. This strategy can create an incentive to diversify and more extensively utilize capital resources. Banks are obligated by law to collateralize tax accounts and certain trust accounts with T-bills. The futures market, which allows them to improve yield, also provides them the safety and liquidity of the T-bill market.

CONSTRUCTION COMPANIES

Builders, developers, and other users of short-term construction loans can use the treasury bill futures market to limit the cost of borrowed money. Short-term construction loans are generally tied to the prime rate until the structure is completed and long-term financing is in place. An increase in the prime rate could push the cost of financing beyond the capacity of the borrower to incur the debt. The risk can be effectively removed by a short hedge. For example, on May 1 a builder anticipates borrowing $2 million for six months on August 15 at a rate of one point over prime. Fearing that the prime may go up by August, he sells two August futures contracts now. If he is correct and interest rates do go up, the inverse relationship of rate and price would cause price to go down. Therefore, he could buy back his two futures contracts in August for a lower price. The gain he realizes in the August futures market will help to offset the increased rate of interest he must pay on his construction loan.

FINANCE COMPANIES

Many finance companies handle the short-term financing of receivables by issuing commercial paper. It is either sold on a discount basis or sold at par and is redeemable at face value plus interest at maturity. Because the interest rate on commercial paper is closely correlated with the rate on treasury bills, this type of borrowing exposure can be hedged effectively in the T-bill futures market. Assume, for example, that a finance company has $5 million in commercial paper outstanding that matures in four months. The treasurer feels that interest rates will go up significantly in this period but decides to "roll over" the paper at maturity anyway. The treasurer, after making this decision to refinance, can go to the futures market and lock in the rate he will have to pay by selling (five) contracts for the month nearest the maturity date of the commercial paper. If his forecast is correct and interest rates do rise, the futures price will fall by a corresponding amount and the contracts can be bought back at the lower price. The profit realized in this transaction will help to offset the increased rate of interest required to roll over the commercial paper. Retailers, manufacturers, and industrial corporations that issue commercial paper could also find T-bill futures a valuable means of minimizing the cost of short-term borrowing.

IMPORT/EXPORT COMPANIES

Any corporation or individual involved in financing foreign and domestic trade is familiar with the bankers' acceptance. This money market instrument is a draft—an order to pay, which a bank guarantees—made by a buyer who does not wish to pay for imported goods until they arrive. The draft is written for a larger amount than was actually borrowed. This discount, or difference, is the interest that is payable at maturity. Because interest rates on bankers' acceptances move in close tandem with T-bill rates, any exposure in BAs can easily be hedged in the T-bill futures market.

For instance, assume a bicycle company ordered some parts from Japan in January for delivery in June. The buyer knows that the seller will want payment when he ships the parts; to satisfy the seller, a bankers' acceptance would be sent to Japan in May. The buyer believes that interest rates will be higher in May so he sells a T-bill contract in January while rates are lower and, therefore, prices are higher. If his forecast is correct, interest rates will go up, futures prices will come down, and the importer will offset his position by buying back his futures contract at a lower price. The profit on the hedge will offset the higher interest rate demanded by the bank that accepts the draft.

THE FINANCIAL MARKET FORMULAS

Normal trading practice among dealers and in the Federal Reserve's weekly auction requires quotes to be based on the bank discount rate, which is also the T-bill yield—the phrases are used interchangeably. But because the bank discount rate is calculated in a unique fashion, a person attempting to equate T-bill yields with bond yields must convert the T-bill rate to a bond equivalent rate.

Essentially, the bank discount rate is the difference between the face value of a bill and its market value on an annualized basis. Formulas for determining price, T-bill yield (bank discount rate), and equivalent bond yield follow.

1. *To determine the T-bill actual issue price:*

$$\$1,000,000 - \frac{(\text{days to maturity} \times \text{T-bill yield} \times \$1,000,000)}{360} = \text{actual issue price}$$

EXAMPLE: Given 6% T-bill yield on a 91-day bill
$\$1,000,000 - (91 \times .06 \times \$1,000,000) = \$984,833.33$ (issue price)

2. *To determine the T-bill yield when T-bill face value, days to maturity, and actual issue price are known:*

$$\frac{\dfrac{(\text{T-bill face value} - \text{actual issue price}) \times 360}{\text{days to maturity}}}{\text{T-bill face value}} = \text{T-bill yield}$$

EXAMPLE: Given, $1,000,000, 91-day T-bill with actual issue price of $984,833.33

$$\frac{\dfrac{(1,000,000 - \$984,833.33) \times 360}{91}}{\$1,000,000} = 6.00\% \text{ T-bill yield}$$

44

3. T-bill yield to equivalent bond yield:

$$\frac{\dfrac{(\text{T-bill face value} - \text{actual issue price}) \times 365}{\text{days to maturity}}}{\text{actual issue price}} = \text{equivalent bond yield}$$

EXAMPLE:

$$\frac{\dfrac{(\$1,000,000 - \$984,833.33) \times 365}{91}}{\$984,833.33} = 6.18\% \text{ equivalent bond}$$

can be used to find the prices that give the same yield for T-bills of different maturities.

$$\$1,000,000 - \frac{(\text{days to maturity} \times \text{T-bill yield} \times \$1,000,000)}{360}$$

EXAMPLE: Converting 90-day bill at T-bill yield of 6% to 91-day bill at 6%.

90-day bill value = $\$1,000,000 - \dfrac{(90 \times .06 \times \$1,000,000)}{360} = \$985,000.00$

91-day bill value = $\$1,000,000 - \dfrac{(91 \times .06 \times \$1,000,000)}{360} = \$984,833.33$

8

Certificates of Deposit
Futures Trading

The new certificates of deposit (CDs) futures are a promise to buy or sell, at a specific price at some specified future date, a $1-million 3-month certificate of deposit issued by one of the top ten American banks.

HISTORY OF
THE CASH CD MARKET

Certificates of deposit, or more accurately large negotiable CDs, were invented by banks in the early 1960s. The banks were hungry for cash. CDs were meant to tap the corporations' short-term surplus funds—money that corporations had kept largely in the form of low-yield treasury securities before the advent of CDs. Both the banks and corporations had used Treasury debt to adjust their balance sheets to accommodate their surplus short-term funding, and neither banks nor corporations were particularly happy with the yield on treasuries.

The instrument has been tremendously successful. Banks learned that they could go beyond their original plan of using CDs to find unexpected surges in loan demand and deposit runoff. CDs became a means of *permanently* increasing the size of the major money center banks. The concept of managing the size of the bank with CDs has come to be known as liability management. All "wholesale" banks today perceive themselves as liability managers.

For the corporate customers of banks, CDs provided both a higher yield and added flexibility, compared to treasuries.

CDs could be written to mature on the day the corporation planned to spend the money, a service the Treasury does not provide. In the event of an unanticipated need for cash, the CD could be resold into the secondary market. The problem with CDs is that the secondary market is not particularly efficient, compared to the treasury bill market. One reason is the lack of homogeneity—CDs are a complex mix of different maturity dates and cash values. This is largely the result of tailoring CDs to the maturity needs of each particular corporate customer. Worse yet, because banks do not issue CDs at predictable times and with specific maturities, it is practically impossible to short a CD. This makes dealing or trading in CDs a risky activity.

1974: The Flight to Quality

There was the leak of the "Problem Bank List" maintained by the Federal Reserve. Investors panicked, selling CDs and buying treasury bills.

Soon thereafter, the emergence of several major cities' financial problems created yet another change in the spread between CDs and T-bills. Money center banks have traditionally maintained relatively large inventories of local municipal obligations, both because of a desire to support their city and because banks alone among institutional investors may borrow to finance the purchase of municipal obligations. Worst of all, major bank failures were beginning to occur, and the overall question of financial strength was raised.

These events, coupled with the high level of short-term rates, were the last straw. CD rates rose and CD/T-bill spreads reached unprecedented levels. Some banks simply could not sell CDs at any price. Other banks bought the CDs of still other banks to take advantage of the high yields.

Recent History of the CD/T-Bill Spread

Although 1974 was an extreme, it is common to see CD rates rise by more than T-bill rates when rates in general are rising.

In periods of rising rates, banks pay an increasingly higher rate relative to the Treasury for two reasons.

1. Banks need the cash to fund the strong loan demand typical of a rising rate environment. At the same time, strong tax revenues usually reduce the Treasury's appetite for cash.

2. Unlike the Treasury, banks cannot issue unlimited amounts of CDs. Banks are subject to credit limits from the buyers of CDs, whereas the government is only limited by the amount of money it needs and unlimited as to the price to pay.

In 1980 interest-rate volatility created a similar increase in the volatility of the spread between CD and T-bill rates as well. In contrast, between 1975 and 1978 the relationship between changes in CD and T-bill rates showed low correlation. That is, a change in the treasury bill rate was not particularly likely to coincide with a change in the CD rate. On the other hand, changes in the spread between T-bill rates and CD rates were relatively small.

TRACKING THE CD/T-BILL SPREAD: THE POWER OF THE SPREAD AND THE PLAY IN THE SPREAD

Two useful measures of the interaction between the CD and T-bill markets are:

1. *The power of the spread*—the odds that CD rates and T-bill rates will rise or fall in tandem.
2. *The play in the spread*—the odds that the CD/T-bill spread will change.

Using this approach, Table 1 compares the power and the play for the CD/T-bill spread in the period before and after the Fed's change in operating procedures. Both the power and the play have increased since October 1979.

TABLE 1. The Power of the Spread and the Play in the Spread

Time Period	Power of the Spread*	Play in the Spread†
Jan. 1975–Sept. 1979	.70	22 basis points
Oct. 1979–Dec. 1980	.90	44 basis points

*Power of the spread, defined as R^2 for regression of month-end to month-end data.
†Play in the spread is the average absolute error for the same regressions.

CD FUTURES VS. CD CASH

Two strategies using both cash and futures markets in CDs to accomplish two critical investment goals, high return and a maximum of flexibility in controlling cash flow, are described in this section. These two examples focus on the unique properties of the CD contract.

Cash and Carry
in the CD Market

Most research on cash and futures yield curves for treasury bills indicates that the yield curve for 90-day T-bill futures is below the cash yield curve. In other words, futures bills are more expensive than bills bought on the implied forward cash basis.

The tendency for cash and futures yield curves to differ in T-bills is not surprising because, except for the front month, there is no existing deliverable bill. Therefore, the disparity between cash and futures rates cannot be arbitraged away. With CDs, however, any delivery bank can create a deliverable CD at any time. Thus, it is interesting to investigate the possible costs and benefits of doing so. If the two yield curves do differ, the time-honored principle "buy low, sell high" suggests that an alternative 3-month investment with the same economic effect as the purchase of a 3-month CD would tend to have a higher yield than the simple purchase of a 3-month CD. With the second transaction, the investor could purchase a 6-month CD and sell a CD futures contract for delivery three months after the purchase.

We constructed hypothetical CD futures yields to determine what effect a CD futures contract would have had on the attractiveness of the cash and carry strategy, compared to owning a CD maturing on the delivery date. The prices of the hypothetical contract were based on the cash price of CDs, but with the yield curves identical to that of the T-bill futures yield curve. In other words, CD futures prices were assumed to differ from T-bill futures prices by the same amount that spot CDs differ from spot T-bill yields, but the slope of the CD futures yield curve was the same as the slope of the T-bill futures contract. All CD futures contract prices, however, were closed out at cash CD yields.

The results indicate that the risk and return of using this strategy was more advantageous to the investor than owning the shorter maturity CD. The yield on a 6-month CD with a hypothetical short CD futures position had a maximum gain of 91 points during any single 3-month period, compared to CDs maturing on the delivery date. In every quarter it outperformed the cash-only transaction. The average gain for every 3-month period was 53 points.

In fact, the systematically positive yield of using this strategy would have been known by the trader at the time of entry. This suggests that prices of the 3-month and 6-month CDs would have to adjust to reduce the relative advantage of buying 6-month CDs and shorting them. Thus, the yield curve for cash CDs will be flatter, making the issuing of longer maturity CDs more attractive. While the arbitrage described in the example will no longer be profitable, the flatter yield curve should result in an expansion in the average maturity of bank CDs issued.

TABLE 2. Using Futures to Shrink a 6-Month CD

Month-End Date	3-Month CD	6-Month CD, Short CD Futures
Nov. 78	10.67	11.41
Feb. 79	10.15	11.01
May 79	10.05	10.54
Aug. 79	11.30	11.79
Nov. 79	13.125	13.545
Feb. 80	15.80	16.71
May 80	8.90	8.95
Aug. 80	11.30	11.60
Nov. 80	17.20	

Max. Gain: .91
Min. Gain: .05
Avg. Gain: .53

A USE OF CD FUTURES FOR CORPORATE TREASURERS: DELIVERY ON THE TAX DATE

One of the big problems for banks in the CD market is that corporations all want CDs that mature on a particular day, the tax date. Up to $2 billion worth of CDs have matured on tax dates to provide corporations with ready cash. This aspect of the CD market is undesirable to banks, although banks do charge the buyers for the problems these CDs create. Corporations typically receive CDs maturing on tax dates at lower yields than nontax-dated CDs.

The CD futures contract may help to solve this problem. A corporate customer of a bank can use the CD futures to guarantee itself receipt of cash on the tax date without requiring the bank to part with funds on the tax date. The contract permits delivery to commence on the fifteenth of the month and delivers CDs maturing on or after the sixteenth of the month three months hence. Therefore, the first delivery day is always a tax date, but the deliverable CD may mature on days other than the tax date. By selling a corporate customer a deliverable CD and allowing him to short the futures contract, the bank has guaranteed available funds on the tax date for the corporate depositor without having to actually supply the funds. An example of this transaction is detailed in Table 3 for July 29, the first day of CD trading.

TABLE 3. Tax Date Hedge

Date: July 29	Cash Market: Buy Dec 16 CD at 18% Invoice price: $1,000,000 Principal plus interest at maturity = $1,000,000 (1 + $\frac{140}{360}$ (.18)) = $1,070,000	Futures Market: Short CD futures at 17.48%
Sept. 15	Delivery CD	Close out short position by delivery

Net Earnings	$\dfrac{\$1,070,000}{(1 + \frac{91}{360}(.1748))}$ $\$1,024,722$	

Add-on Return	$\dfrac{\$1,024,722}{(1 + \frac{49}{360}(.1748))} = 18.16$	

USING FUTURES TO MANAGE RISKS ASSOCIATED WITH OTHER MONEY MARKET INSTRUMENTS

CD Futures and Floating-Rate Euroloans

The floating-rate Euroloan is a popular vehicle for bank-financed capital expenditures. These loans are long-term commitments, but the interest cost is readjusted quarterly at the prevailing London interbank offer rate (LIBOR) on the day the rate is reset. As Table 4 shows, CDs are closely related to Eurodollars.

TABLE 4. The Eurodollar/CD Spread and the Eurodollar/T-Bill Spread

Instrument	Hedge Ratio	Power of the Spread*	Play of the Spread
CD	0.98	0.98	28 basis points
T-bill	1.13	0.92	52 basis points

This relationship is even stronger than the relationship between treasury bills and Eurodollars.

CD futures may be used by corporate borrowers in the Euro-market to protect themselves from the possibility that Eurodollar rates might rise. The following example describes the performance of a hedge of a 6-month floating-rate Eurodollar loan, written at the end of August 1980.

TABLE 5. Floating Euroloan Hedge

Date	Cash Market	Futures Market
Aug. 31	Cost of Loan: 12.313	Dec. CD Futures Yield: 12.05*
Nov. 30	Cost of Loan: 18.125	Dec. CD Futures Yield: 15.53

TOTAL INTEREST EXPENSE: 15.216
GAIN FROM CD FUTURES: 3.480
NET COST OF FUNDS: 13.479

*Futures prices were constructed by using the cash CD rate and deriving the futures yield from the line with the same slope as the T-bill futures yield curve.

USING CD FUTURES TO HEDGE 1-MONTH COMMERCIAL PAPER

Although CD futures trade based on delivery of a 90-day instrument, they also can be effective when used with other short-term instruments. Table 6 shows the relationship between 30-day commercial paper and 3-month CDs, as well as the relationship between 30-day commercial paper and 90-day T-bills. The table indicates a strong relationship between changes in 30-day commercial paper rates and changes in 90-day CDs when measured every three months.

TABLE 6. Changes in 30-Day Commercial Paper Rates Compared to 3-Month CDs and T-Bills

Instrument	Hedge Ratio	Power	Play
CD	0.90	0.97	25 basis points
T-bill	1.03	0.89	55 basis points

Table 7 shows the results of rolling over 1-month commercial paper during a 6-month period by using 3-month CD futures. As the table demonstrates, the cost of funds in the commercial paper market was protected largely by CD futures during this period.

TABLE 7. Commercial Paper Hedge

Date	Cash Market	Futures Market	
		Sept.	Dec.
June 30		Sell at 8.89	Sell at 9.09
July 31	9.900	Buy Back at 10.36	
Aug. 31	10.675	Buy Back at 11.75	
Sept. 30	12.700		Buy Back at 12.98
Oct. 31	13.125		Buy Back at 14.65
Nov. 30	16.590		17.03

NET COST OF FUNDS
June—8.889
July—8.430
Aug.—7.815
Sept.—8.810
Oct.—7.565
Nov.—8.650

AVERAGE COST OF FUNDS: 11.979
AVERAGE COST OF FUTURES GAIN: 3.620
NET COST OF FUNDS: 8.359

THE CD FUTURES CONTRACT: TERMS OF THE CONTRACT AND COMPARISON TO CASH QUOTES

Pricing the CD Futures Contract

There is an important distinction between the formula for the invoice price of a $1-million CD and the formula for the invoice price of a $1-million 90-day treasury bill. Formula (1) below is for computing the invoice price of a 90-day treasury bill.

(1)   Invoice price $= (1 - \frac{90}{360}$ [F yield] million)

where F yield $= 100.00$ (IMM index on last trading day)

In this formula the yield results in a deduction from the basic $1-million maturity value of the deliverable time deposit. For this reason the yield is called a *discount* yield. Formula (2), on the other hand, describes the relationship between the invoice price and the maturity value (principal plus interest at maturity) of a deliverable CD.

(2)   Invoice price $=$ (maturity value) $\div (1 + \frac{90}{360}$ [F yield])

In this instance the maturity value, usually greater than $1 million, is divided by 1 plus the futures yield on the deliverable CD at the close on the last day of trading. Since the maturity value exceeds the invoice price, which is typically a multiple of $1 million, this yield is called an *add-on* yield.

Consider the meaning of a 14 percent yield on a 90-day treasury bill and the same 14 percent yield on an add-on CD issued with 90 days to maturity. In the case of the 90-day bill, the bank discount yield of 14 percent means that the treasury bill has an initial value of $965,600, $35,000 less than the maturity value of the bill, which is $1 million. On the other hand, a $1-million CD with a bank add-on yield of 14 percent has a maturity value of $1,035,000, $35,000 more than its initial value of

$1 million. The IMM provides, on request, a booklet that compares add-on yields to discount yields for 90-day instruments.

The delivery process for domestic CDs is different from that of the treasury bill contract. In the case of the treasury bill contract, there is a single delivery day, the issue date of the deliverable 91-day bill (although late deliveries based on a 91-day invoice price are permitted on the two following business days). The delivery period in the case of the CD is much longer, from the first business day following the fifteenth day of the delivery month to the end of the month. This is to facilitate redeliveries of a given outstanding amount of secondary deliverable CDs. In order to maximize the number of CDs that are deliverable, the contract has a large "window" of CDs deliverable. Any CD, of an approved delivery bank, written to mature during the second half of the month, three calendar months from the delivery date, is deliverable. The combined effect of the long period for deliveries and the window of deliverable CDs is that CDs between 2½ and 3½ months to maturity could be delivered. With the one-month window, the magnitude of the deliverable supply is roughly $5 billion, comparable to the deliverable supply on the IMM's 90-day T-bill contract.

The Exchange has attempted to facilitate the trading of CD futures by taking advantage of factors the CD market has in common with the T-bill cash market in designing the CD contract. For example, the CD will be quoted on an index basis (100 = yield) just like the T-bill; and the delivery period for the CD includes the delivery dates for the 90-day T-bill futures contract.

There are some differences, however, and these differences are critical to understanding the pricing of the new CD contract. The two primary differences are:

1. The CD index is based on an add-on yield, not a discount yield, so the yields must be "translated" into comparable terms.

2. The CD has a half-month delivery period, not a single-day delivery like the T-bill, in order to assure sufficient deliverable supply, since unlike bills, CDs are not issued on one particular day.

Add-On Yields vs. Discount Yields

The cash and futures markets for CDs are markets for an instrument quoted on a bank add-on basis, which is not a yield directly comparable to the discount yield found in the cash and futures markets for T-bills. The CD Futures Yields Calculator enables traders to compare these two yields.

A $1-million seasoned CD with an original issue date six months before the maturity date, and with an original bank add-on yield of 9 percent, would have a maturity value of:

$$\text{Maturity value} = (1 + \frac{180}{360}[.09]) (\$1,000,000)$$

$$= \$1,045,000$$

Suppose this particular seasoned CD were deliverable with 90 days remaining to maturity at a futures price of 88.50 (yielding 11.50 percent), the invoice price would equal:

$$\frac{\$1,045,000}{(1 + \frac{90}{360}[.115])} = \$1,015,795.80$$

The formula for the discount yield of the same CD on the same day is:

$$(\$1,045,000) (1 - \frac{90}{360}[X]) = \$1,015,795.80$$

with solution $X = 11.18$

Thus, the discount yield associated with an add-on yield of 11.50 percent is 11.18 percent.

Thus far, we have discussed trading techniques in treasury bills and certificates of deposit. Of course, it is also possible to trade in treasury bonds.

The simplest strategy is to buy a bill or bond contract with a June delivery date while selling a contract with a September delivery date. This is called a bull spread, because the price of both bills and bonds is expected to go up. The spread is just in case prices do not go up.

Spread trading is baffling in its complexity and not as risk-free as some brokers might suggest. The offsetting position of buying a contract while selling a similar one may look like a prudent hedge. If rates move in tandem, as they often do, a loss in one contract will be compensated partly by a gain in the other, no matter which is moving faster. But if one contract price is rallying while the other is flat, or, worse, the yield differential in a bull spread is widening rather than narrowing, losses can be sharp and even deeper than a one-contract position.

For a further discussion of financial futures trading techniques, including the GNMA market (FHA and VA mortgage guarantee program), the reader is referred to *Inside the Financial Futures Markets*, by Mark J. Powers and David J. Vogel (New York: Wiley, 1981).

9

Foreign Exchange Futures

THE SYSTEM
OF INTERNATIONAL PAYMENTS

If you buy a pound of hamburger at the corner grocery store, you will naturally want to pay for it with dollars, and the grocer will want to be paid in dollars because he pays all his bills with dollars. Likewise, if a British citizen wants kidney pie for dinner, he purchases the kidneys at the butcher shop and pays for them in pounds sterling. The butcher is happy because he meets his expenses with sterling.

However, if an American developed a taste for kidney pie and wished to purchase the kidneys directly from a butcher shop in England, the transaction would become somewhat more complicated. He would like to pay in dollars, but the butcher would want pounds. Somehow the American would have to acquire pounds if he wished to indulge his craving for kidney pie.

In the world today there are millions of such transactions between citizens of different countries. A system of exchange rates has evolved to facilitate such trade. Exchange rates are nothing more than the "price" of a foreign currency in terms of one's own currency.

Evolution of Money
and International Payments

Early in man's recorded history, precious metals were used as money. Eventually, gold evolved as the primary precious metal used. Men have been assigning value to gold for thousands of years. In early societies gold coins replaced barter and became legal tender. Gold didn't really enter the money system in a major way until 1816, when Great Britain became the first country to fix the value of an ounce of gold in terms of the pound sterling, and gold became the major means of settling international debts. Gradually, other countries followed suit. In 1900 the U.S. dollar was fixed in terms of gold at $20.67 a troy ounce. With the election of President Franklin D. Roosevelt, during the Great Depression, the price of gold in terms of the dollar was fixed on a daily basis until it was set at $35 to the troy ounce of gold in 1934. Concurrent with this fixing, American citizens were restricted from owning the precious metal. December 31, 1974, marked the first time since then that gold bullion was legally holdable by private citizens.

In order to better understand the evolution of money, let's assume that the United States Government minted a gold piece with the American eagle stamped on it and called it one "dollar." This one-dollar gold piece contained precisely $1/20$ of an ounce of gold. At the same time the King of England created a gold piece containing $1/4$ of an ounce of gold, stamped his likeness on the face, and called it, of all things, a "pound."

The pound, therefore, contained five times as much gold as the dollar $(1/20 \times 5 = 1/4)$.

If an American wished to trade his dollars for sterling, he would have to put up five dollars to receive one pound. This would mean the "price" of the pound to the American was five dollars. This "price" would be the exchange rate.

In time gold became cumbersome and governments began to create paper certificates or coins of cheaper metal that were redeemable for gold. A U.S. dollar paper certificate could be taken to the United States Treasury and exchanged for $1/20$ of an ounce of gold.

As world trade increased, governments printed more and more paper certificates. Soon there were more paper certificates than there was gold in a country's treasury. If everyone came to the treasury at once and demanded gold for his or her certificates, the coffers would be empty before each one had received his or her gold. Although no major government has had such a run on its gold supply, the mere knowledge of the possibility of such pressing demands caused the value of the paper certificate to decrease. If there were 1 million one-dollar paper certificates in the world and only $900,000 worth of gold in Fort Knox, people would soon believe each dollar they held was only worth $.90 (900,000 ÷ 1,000,000).

In reality it did not work this way. One dollar was still worth one dollar to all citizens of the United States transacting business within the United States. But when they wished to do business with a British citizen, they would have to pay more than five dollars to receive one pound if they were to receive equivalent gold backing (assuming, of course, that the King of England had not issued more pound notes than he had in gold in his coffers). Thus, the "price," or exchange rate, in this case, would increase.

As time passed, paper certificates became acceptable as money, regardless of how much gold was behind them, because people knew that stable governments would stand behind their currency. The fact that the certificates were backed by something of value made them acceptable as money.

Paper currencies throughout the world have evolved to the point where nearly all governments have many more paper certificates than they have gold.

On August 15, 1971, the United States government officially stopped redeeming paper certificates for gold. In reality the practice had ceased some time earlier. However, there had never been an "official" announcement.

This certainly did not cause the world to stop turning. The old laws of supply and demand, which had been gaining influence with the increase of "paper money," began to play a larger role. Gold had served its function by establishing the rate of exchange between countries. Supply and demand are now important factors in the fluctuations above and below that rate. Many eminent economists and knowledgeable people feel that we will return to gold backing. However, this does not affect the logic of international payments. For purposes of explanation, we can disregard gold and think in terms of supply and demand.

The laws of supply and demand for currency can best be explained by an example. If foreigners are eager to buy U.S. goods, they will be eager to buy U.S. dollars to pay for those goods. This increased demand for U.S. dollars will drive the price up for foreigners. If a Briton can "buy" U.S. dollars at the rate of .5882 pounds/dollar (the reciprocal of $1.70/pound), the increased demand may drive the "price" up to, say, .5995 pounds/dollar. The "price" for dollars in terms of British pounds could rise to a point at which Britons' tastes for American goods are overridden.

Such an increased demand could affect the "price" of any currency. The supply side of the coin could also cause exchange-rate fluctuations. If the supply of dollars held by foreigners is large, its "price" will decrease. This law of supply and demand is thus a basic force influencing the fluctuation of exchange rates.

IMF Agreements and Par Values

The system of international payments was formalized in 1944 with the creation of the International Monetary Fund at Bretton Woods, New Hampshire. This meeting of the major industrialized countries of the West established a pay value for the major currencies vis-a-vis the U.S. dollar, then pegged at $35 to the troy ounce of gold. The fluctuation limits were set at 1 percent above or below the par value for cash, or "spot," transactions only. This system worked reasonably well for a number of years. As long as the United States was willing to run its balance of payments at a deficit, the system continued. The volume of dollars overseas increased as the United States purchased foreign automobiles, fine wines, and other items from our trading partners. With this huge supply of U.S. dollars abroad, they naturally became overvalued. Shortly after the first U.S. devaluation in 1971, the IMF meeting in Washington, D.C., allowed those limits to expand to 2¼ percent either side of par. This Smithsonian Agreement, in allowing greater fluctuation around the parity level, necessitated greater hedging activity by commercial interests.

With the Smithsonian meeting concluded, the creation of the IMM was announced. It was determined that, with the larger fluctuation limits, the feasibility of starting a futures market in foreign exchange could be established. However, before discussing the IMM further, we should consider the method by which the developed countries controlled parity.

One method the IMF member countries used to maintain the spot rates of exchange within limits was central bank intervention. Even today, with the so-called free-floating system, we have what is sometimes referred to as a "dirty float," whereby the central banks will intervene. Central banks have semiofficial status within federal governments and are used in fulfillment of fiscal and monetary policy.

If it were assumed for explanatory purposes that supply and demand were the only factors considered by central banks, if the price of a country's currency rose to its upper intervention limit, then central banks would take steps to increase the supply of that currency and thereby drive its "price" down. They would do this by selling their own currency and taking foreign currency in payment. If the exchange rate were at the lower intervention limit, a central bank would buy its own currency in an attempt to decrease the supply and thereby drive the "price" up.

Par values were changed from time to time in an effort to keep the fixed rate in line with reality. Obviously, it could be very expensive for a government to attempt to maintain an exchange rate that was far out of line with a rate that would be set by marked influences such as supply and demand.

THE MODERN
FOREIGN EXCHANGE MARKET

The Spot Market

It was mentioned earlier that millions of currency transactions take place daily between citizens of different countries. Since it would be extremely difficult for someone who needed pounds sterling to search out an individual who has them for sale, the foreign exchange market has developed as a medium through which buyers and sellers can readily get in touch with each other. Historically, banks have handled this service. Through their correspondent relationships with banks in various countries, they have easy access to foreign currency. Naturally, there is not a physical transfer of, let's say, Swiss francs for U.S. dollars. It is simply a bookkeeping entry whereby the bank in the United States and the bank in Switzerland credit each other's account for the currency. The U.S. bank keeps an account with the Swiss bank, and vice versa. They then exchange a dollar balance in the U.S. bank for a Swiss franc balance in the Swiss bank. Another way of considering the bank transaction is a swap of IOUs.

At any rate, any bank dealing in foreign exchange can, in a very short time, provide any customer with an exchange rate for any currency. For example, if a customer called a bank in Chicago and asked for 250,000 Swiss francs, the bank would call two or three or more foreign currency dealers, via direct line, and get the cheapest price available for 250,000 Swiss francs. The bank may just happen to have a Swiss franc balance in its account already and may elect to sell those francs out of its own inventory. In any case, the customer will have, in very short order, the Swiss francs he requested. He may also have the bank, for a small fee, deliver the francs to any bank of his choosing via cable transfer or mail.

This market is somewhat akin to the over-the-counter market in securities. There is no centralized meeting place and no fixed opening and closing time. In fact, some foreign exchange dealers in London banks maintain a twenty-four-hour-a-day operation. Furthermore, there are no requirements for participating except informal acceptance of an unwritten code of financial and moral conduct.

The banks do the majority of the foreign exchange business, but there are other participants. Some large multinational firms maintain extensive foreign exchange trading departments. There are currently a few wholesale brokers in New York and other large financial centers who buy and sell large blocks of foreign exchange among the banks at very small margins. There are also a few brokers who deal in foreign exchange at the retail level, that is, with speculators or with hedgers other than banks.

Forward Market Among Banks

In addition to changing money, the foreign exchange dealers regularly sell various currencies for forward deliveries. Most banks that deal in foreign exchange can enter into a contract to buy or sell any amount of a currency at any date in the future—that is, for forward delivery—for its customers. Some limitations to such transactions are (1) the ability of the bank to find a customer for the opposite side of the transaction, (2) willingness of the bank to take the opposite side itself, if necessary, and (3) the credit-worthiness of the customer. Banks normally like to balance out their obligations in the forward and cash markets. Since they are not basically risk-seeking institutions, they attempt to "hedge" all their transactions. In times of increased uncertainty, this fact may hinder a bank's ability to provide forward sales or purchases of currency.

Overall, the modern foreign exchange market has been beneficial in promoting world trade. Although few in number, the banks involved are large. It is estimated that approximately $450–500 billion a year in foreign exchange are traded in the United States.

HEDGING IN THE FUTURES MARKET

Hedging may be defined as the purchase or sale of a futures contract as a temporary substitute for a future cash transaction. It also may be the purchase or sale of a futures contract to offset an equal and opposite transaction or position in the cash market. It is anticipated that by such a transaction any loss in one market will be offset by a gain in the other and thus loss through price change will be significantly reduced.

The purpose of a hedge is to protect the operating profit anticipated through the normal course of business. Speculative profit results solely from changes in price and is not the result of a manufacturing or marketing function. Importers are primarily interested in selling their imported goods at a profit. They prefer to leave the assumption of foreign exchange risk to some other person who willingly accepts that risk in hope of profit by correctly anticipating "price" movements. That other person is the speculator, who was discussed earlier.

The essence of effective hedging is the *basis* and its movement. The basis in this context is the difference between the cash, or spot, exchange rate and the futures exchange rate.

In actuality the basis tends toward zero as the delivery day for the futures contract approaches. This is reasonable because, in the end, the futures delivery becomes a spot delivery. They become perfect substitutes for each other, hence they should have equal value. This principle is very important in a futures market, since it is the essence of the use of the futures for "forward pricing," or fixing of costs in advance.

In foreign exchange the basis primarily reflects (1) the interest-rate differential among countries and (2) expectations. If stable conditions exist and there are not restrictions for trade and capital flow, forward rates will vary inversely with the interest-rate differential between two countries. For example, if interest rates are 2 percent higher in Canada than in the United States, the forward price for Canadian dollars should be at a 2 percent discount in terms of U.S. dollars. This is called interest-rate parity and is explained in detail later.

Since world monetary conditions have been relatively unstable, and barriers to free trade do exist, interest-rate parity is seldom achieved. Expectations have played a larger role. Nevertheless, interest-rate parity is a starting point for analyzing the basis.

There has also been an identifiable seasonal trend in the basis of some currencies, roughly coinciding with peak export and import seasons.

The following examples will help to illustrate hedging procedures, although it must be borne in mind that in actual practice the hedges may not work out as close to perfection as these.

Example 1: Selling Hedge

United States Banker

In a straight *selling hedge* a *long*, or *buy*, position is taken in the *spot* market at the same time that the opposition position—that is, a *short*, or *sell*, position—is taken in the *futures* market.

For example, one might assume that a bank in Chicago has excess funds to invest short-term, and the highest short-term interest rate is currently being paid in Canada. Say 91-day Canadian treasury bills are yielding 6.0 percent and U.S. treasury bills are yielding 5.5 percent. The Chicago banker will *buy* Canadian treasury bills. At the same time he will *sell* Canadian dollars in the futures market for delivery three months hence. The number of Canadian dollars he sells in the futures market will include the original number plus the interest that will accrue.

The advantage of the hedge is that he has fixed his selling price for the Canadian dollar 91 days from now. This way he can be assured that the interest income on the treasury bills will not be lost in the conversion back to U.S. dollars if the price for Canadian dollars goes down during the period. The transaction may be summarized as follows:

Cash Market		Futures Market	
Dec. 1			
Bought 191,000 CD @ $.9800/CD	$187,180	Sold 200,000 Mar. CD @ $.9810	$196,200
Mar. 1			
Sold 191,000 CD @ $.9600/CD	$183,360	Bought (offset) Mar. CD @ $.9601	$192,020
Loss	$ 3,820	Gain	$ 4,180
Sold interest accrued ($11,460 @ 6% annualized) on CD treasury bills @ $.9600/CD = $11,001.60 ÷ 4 = $2.750.40 for 90 days			

In this example, the banker, if he had *not* hedged, would have lost $1,069.60 on his transaction ($3,820.00 − $2,750.40 = $1,069.60) when he changed his CD back to U.S. dollars because the spot price of CD went down. However, by hedging in the futures market, he actually recovered all of his interest income in the futures transaction, and made a small profit of $360 on the hedge as well ($4,180 − $3,820 = $360). He could just as easily have lost a small amount. The important point is that the hedge protected his interest income from the exchange risk.

Example 2: Selling Hedge

Multinational Company

A multinational company may also have need for a selling hedge. Suppose a Chicago tractor manufacturer has a plant in Switzerland. The Swiss plant is short of funds to meet payroll expenses. In six months, at the peak of the farm-machinery buying season, it expects to be in a sound position again. The logical move for the Chicago parent company is to transfer the necessary funds to the Swiss plant for six months. At the end of that period, the Swiss plant would return the funds to the Chicago office. The arithmetic of such a transaction would look like this:

Cash Market		Futures Market	
June 1			
Bought 500,000 SF @ $.4015	$200,750	Sold 500,000 Dec. SF @ $.4060	$203,000
Dec. 1			
Sold 500,000 SF @ $.4060	$203,000	Bought (offset) Dec. SF @ $.4065	$203,250
GAIN	$ 2,250	LOSS	$ 250

In this example the hedger had a profit in the cash market of $2,250 and a loss in the futures market of $250. This small loss of $250 in the futures market represents ⅛ of 1 percent of the entire transaction. Had the cash market gone down by the same amount, the tractor maker would have lost the entire $2,250 amount had he *not* been hedged. The important point is that the tractor maker was protected by his hedge against any significant loss through an adverse exchange-rate fluctuation.

Example 3: Buying Hedge

Multinational Company

In a *buying hedge* the currency is *sold* in the *spot* market and is *bought* in the *futures* market. It is the opposite of a selling hedge.

In this example assume the Chicago tractor manufacturer's Swiss plant is doing very well and has excess funds in the form of Swiss francs. It has no use for these funds until Swiss taxes are due in six months. At the same time, the Chicago tractor maker has an engine plant in Peoria that is desperately in need of short-term funds to meet operating expenses. The best move for the tractor maker would be to transfer those funds from the Swiss plant to the Peoria plant for six months. In this transaction the hedger would sell the spot Swiss francs and buy Swiss francs on the IMM for future delivery—a buying hedge. Here is how the transaction would look:

Cash Market		Futures Market	
June 1			
Bought 500,000 SF @ $.4015	$200,750	Sold 500,000 Dec. SF @ $.4060	$203,000
Dec. 1			
Sold 500,000 SF @ $.4100	$205,000	Sold (offset) Dec. SF @ $.4110	$205,500
LOSS	$ 4,250	GAIN	$ 2,500

In this example prices moved up sharply, as they actually did in June and July of 1977. This time the hedger has a loss of $4,250 in the cash market that was partially offset by a gain of $2,500 in the futures market.

FORWARD PRICING

Goods and services are normally paid for in the currency of the seller. This may be a negotiated item between buyer and seller. If an importer knows he must take delivery on goods valued at 500,000 deutsche marks from West Germany six months hence, he is certain that he will have to deliver 500,000 deutsche marks on that date.

What he does not know at this time is the "price" of the deutsche marks, that is, the exchange rate. He can lock in the cost of those deutsche marks now by purchasing four futures contracts for delivery of 500,000 deutsche marks in that month. He then has hedged his foreign exchange exposure. Whether the rate of exchange for deutsche marks goes up or down, the importer knows what the approximate "price" will be. This is most advantageous to the importer. He makes his profit by distributing his German-made goods in the United States. He does not care, and may not be qualified, to speculate in foreign exchange.

The step-by-step procedure is as follows: On June 1 the importer bids on a contract to take delivery of 100,000 West German widgets to be delivered on December 1, at a price of DM 500,000. On June 1 the deutsche mark is selling for $.4216/DM on the spot market and $.4242/DM for future delivery in the month of December. The importer decides to hedge his exchange risk in the futures market.

When purchasing the December futures contracts in deutsche

marks, the importer knows that the price quoted is for delivery on December 15 (the third Wednesday of the month). The importer will be lifting his hedge on December 1, when he will offset his futures contracts and purchase spot deutsche marks to pay for his widgets. Since futures and spot prices roughly coincide only on the last trading day, as discussed at the beginning of the chapter, the importer would expect the basis (difference between cash and futures) to have narrowed from the June 1 basis, but not to have disappeared.

The importer, being an astute hedger, interpolates between the cash price for DM on June 1 and the futures price for delivery on December 15. The number he derives from this interpolation is his estimated basis for December 1, six months from now. The arithmetic is as follows:

```
              6 mo.
      [ ——————————————————————————————— ]  Dec. 1
June 1                6½ mo.
      [ ——————————————————————————————— ]  Dec. 15
```

December 1 is $^{12}/_{13}$ of the way between June 1 and December 15. The basis on June 1 is \$.0026/DM (\$.4242/DM−\$.4216/DM). By December 1 that basis should have progressed $^{12}/_{13}$ of the way from 26 "points" to zero, or down to 2 points. In other words, on December 1 the same futures contracts should be above cash by \$.0002/DM. Since the futures price is known, the importer can compute the cash estimate for that day.

Dec. futures	\$.4242/DM
Dec. 1 estimated basis	− \$.0002/DM
Dec.	\$.4240/DM estimated cash price on Dec. 1

This figure of \$.4240 is the figure the importer will use when he makes his bid for the West German widgets. The transaction would look like this:

Cash Market		Futures Market		Basis
June 1				
Anticipated Dec. 1		Bought 500,000		
DM spot price	\$.4240/DM*	Dec. DM @	\$.4242/DM	\$.0002/DM
Dec. 1				
Bought spot		Sold (offset)		
DM @	\$.4257/DM	Dec. DM @	\$.4262/DM	\$.0005/DM
	− \$.0017/DM		+\$.0020/DM	−\$.0003/DM

*Based on December DM futures

It will be noticed that the actual cash price on December 1 for deutsche marks (\$.4257/DM) was quite a bit higher than the estimate of \$.4240/DM.

The basis of $.0002/DM, however, was very close. The actual basis on December 1 was $.0005/DM, or $.0003/DM higher than anticipated. This resulted in a small profit of $.0003/DM on the entire hedge transaction. The importer had anticipated paying $.0002/DM less than futures for his deutsche marks. As it worked out, he paid $.0005 less than futures.

The very small profit on this hedge could just as easily have been a small loss if the importer had overestimated the basis. However, it is a very small amount compared to the loss that would have occurred had the importer not hedged. The cash price for DM went up $.0041/DM ($.4257 − $.4216 = $.0041) over the period. On December 1, then, cash DM would have cost $2,050 more (for 500,000 DM) than they did on June 1. This could have substantially eaten into his profit margin had the importer based his contract bid on the price of June 1 cash DM.

This forward-pricing example utilizes basis estimation as an alternative for actual spot-price forecasting. Because of the relationship between the cash and futures prices, basis estimation is much more reliable than cash-price forecasting.

The exporter may have a need for the hedging facilities of a futures market if he takes payment for his goods in other than U.S. dollars. In this case the exporter, if he were receiving payment in deutsche marks, may sell four futures contracts for delivery in the quarter closest to when he receives payment. The mechanics of the hedge, and the risk protection afforded, are the same as those shown in the selling hedge examples.

The American exporter who contracts to take DM 500,000 for payment of U.S. goods delivered on December 1 would sell four futures contracts in DM, for delivery in December, to fix his exchange cost. He then would know in June his income in December, in U.S. dollars, from the sale of his U.S. goods. He also has hedged his risk in the foreign exchange market.

In both examples the cost of deutsche marks could have decreased or increased. Actually, it increased in value during the June 1– December 1 period. In this case the importer would profit on the futures market, but lose about the same amount in the spot market. Thus, he is still effectively hedged. The exporter who sold the futures contracts would lose on the futures contracts and gain the same amount on the spot market. He, too, is still effectively hedged. Regardless of which way the market goes, the hedger has effectively "fixed" his cost.

Conclusion

The preceding examples may be applied to a variety of actual situations. The following are just a few categories in which futures hedging could be used:

1. Companies building plants abroad
2. Companies financing subsidiaries abroad
3. Manufacturers importing raw materials and exporting finished products
4. Exporters taking payment in foreign currency
5. Companies dealing in goods bought and sold in two foreign countries
6. Companies abroad financing operations in Euro-currencies
7. Stock purchases or sales in foreign countries
8. Purchases or sales of foreign securities

The possibilities are limitless. Virtually everyone who deals in or with foreign countries has a need for this hedging mechanism to avoid major loss due to exchange-rate fluctuations.

FUNDAMENTAL FACTORS OF FOREIGN EXCHANGE

What makes foreign rates fluctuate from day to day? Why does the U.S. dollar buy less in Germany in 1977 than it did in 1962? Would an increase in the general level of interest rates in England be bullish or bearish? For whom?

These questions and many more are of utmost importance to anyone dealing in international trade or foreign exchange. There are no pat answers. The fundamental factors affecting foreign exchange are not independent or static.

III

SPECULATING IN METALS

10

Some Comments
About Speculating

It is not the intention of this text to convince you to speculate in commodities of anything. My feeling is that the would-be investor be continually reminded that commodities are fraught with risk.

To reinforce this point, consider what happens after you've decided you do want to speculate and you've selected a broker. The first order of business your broker undertakes is to have you sign a "Risk Disclosure Statement." This statement is furnished to you because rule 1.55 of the Commodity Futures Trading Commission requires it.

The risk of loss in trading commodity futures contracts can be substantial. You should therefore carefully consider whether such trading is suitable for you in light of your financial condition. In considering whether to trade, you should be aware of the following:

1. You may sustain a total loss of the initial margin funds and any additional funds that you deposit with your broker to establish or maintain a position in the commodity futures market. If the market moves against your position, you may be called upon by your broker to deposit a substantial amount of additional margin funds, on short notice, in order to maintain your position. If you do not provide the required funds within the prescribed time, your position may be liquidated at a loss, and you will be liable for any resulting deficit in your account.

2. Under certain market conditions, you may find it difficult or impossible to liquidate a position. This can occur, for example, when the market makes a "limit move."

3. Placing contingent orders, such as "stop-loss" or "stop-limit" orders, will not necessarily limit your losses to the intended amounts, since market conditions may make it impossible to execute such orders.

4. A "spread" position may not be less risky than a simple "long" or "short" position.

5. The high degree of leverage that is often obtainable in futures trading because of the small margin requirements can work against you as well as for you. The use of leverage can lead to large losses as well as gains.

This brief statement cannot, of course, disclose all the risks and other significant aspects of the commodity markets. You should therefore carefully study futures trading before you trade.

The reader is reminded of the following:

1. Losses can be quite substantial.

2. You can very well lose all original and variation margin. If you run out of margin money, the brokerage could sell your house to satisfy any additional indebtedness.

3. "Stop-loss" or "limit" orders don't necessarily get you out of a losing position.

4. You can lose as much on a "spread" as on an "outright," even though the margin is 50 percent less for a spread.

5. Leverage is a two-way street. It's only attractive if you're on the right side of the market.

Well, if this hasn't frightened you off, let's push ahead with some tales of gold.

11

Speculating in Gold

GOLD—A MONETARY PERSPECTIVE

Gold coins first came into use as the barter system disappeared and, along with silver, continued as a principal money of the world for approximately 3,500 years.

In the seventeenth and eighteenth centuries there was a move away from gold coins toward paper currencies as people deposited their gold with local goldsmiths for safekeeping and received receipts for the amount deposited. These receipts then circulated as money in place of gold itself. With the coming of industrial society and the increased demand for money stocks in order to carry on the expanded commerce, paper came to replace gold for normal, everyday transaction. It was easier to carry than gold, and as long as people accepted paper in lieu of gold, it served as a convenient means of payment.

Great Britain was the first country in modern time to officially tie its paper currency to gold when, in 1816, it fixed the value of an ounce of gold in terms of the pound. Other European countries followed suit, and eventually so did the United States. The U.S. dollar was first fixed in terms of gold in 1900.

Under the original "full" gold standard, the amount of a nation's currency in circulation was closely tied to the amount of gold in the country's reserves, and currency and gold coins moved freely from country to country as nations settled their international trading accounts.

Later, a gold bullion standard existed briefly under which nations redeemed their bank notes with gold bullion rather than with coin. Problems arose with this system, however, and the international community switched to a modified gold exchange standard whereby settlement of international accounts was made in major paper currencies, chiefly the U.S. dollar and the British pound.

Although gold, at least theoretically, remained the underlying base for the gold exchange standard, a number of changes in the international monetary system reduced the importance of gold in practice.

Under the Bretton Woods agreement of 1944, the central banks of the world set up a formal system to keep the U.S. dollar exchange rates for their currencies within a 1 percent range above or below a declared par value. In addition, they agreed that the U.S. dollar would be the kingpin of the international money system and, as such, convertible into gold at $35 an ounce. This system collapsed in 1971 when the United States, after suffering substantial and continuing losses of gold, refused to continue converting foreign-held dollars into gold, and later twice devalued the dollar. This led to today's widespread floating of major currencies. A two-tier gold market was established in 1968, that is, a private or free market and an "official" rate at which the price of gold was pegged for making international payments among countries' central banks. But the extensive floating of currencies further diminished the role of the precious metal in the conduct of such transactions.

Beginning in June 1976, however, the International Monetary Fund, which was established in 1947 as an agency of the United Nations to foster international monetary cooperation, has held monthly auctions of gold. The "profit" from these auctions is the difference between the IMF's selling price and the "official" IMF price of $41 an ounce. This profit, about $96 an ounce, had put about $1 billion into the trust fund for sixty-one of the world's less developed nations by the end of 1977. These nations borrow from the fund on easy terms.

Leading members of the IMF reached an agreement in Jamaica in January 1976 under which central banks, starting early in 1978, would be free to buy and sell bullion without restriction at the free-market price, and an IMF amendment put an end to the "official" price of gold. These two actions together effectively and finally demonetized gold.

The London and Zurich Gold Markets

London, with its long-standing ties to South Africa, has always been an important center for dealings in gold. Today, London prices are still watched as price guidelines for the free market in gold.

Five international bullion houses make up the London Gold Market. Representatives of these five firms meet twice daily, at

10:30A.M. and 3:00 P.M. (London time) for the purpose of establishing a morning and afternoon daily price fixing. Bids and offers are brought to the meetings from banking and industrial clients of the five houses. When buy and sell orders can be consumated at a price satisfactory to all, the fixed price has been established. London Gold Market prices serve as a benchmark for private gold dealing throughout the world.

Another world gold-trading center is Zurich. Switzerland has long been a gold-conscious country, and in recent years Zurich has emerged as a major world gold-trading center. During the 1968 world monetary crisis, prior to the establishment of the two-tier system, the London Market was forced to suspend business for a two-week period. The Swiss were quick to take advantage of the vacuum thus created and seized the opportunity to expand their business. Ranking close to London in importance, Zurich continues as a major center for gold dealings.

The Gold Contract

A futures contract for gold is a legally binding instrument to buy or sell a designated quantity of gold at a specific time period in the future, at a price agreed upon today. The contract details the standards the gold must meet in order to be acceptable for delivery. Price is arrived at through an open, competitive auction system.

To enter into a contract, a buyer or seller is required by the brokerage firm and by the exchange to provide a security deposit, usually called margin, which normally is less than 10 percent of the contract's value. These security deposits control large amounts of money at a relatively small cost.

All trades (buying and selling of futures contracts) must be executed by brokers, who perform this service for a nominal commission fee. The procedure of opening an account and entering an order is simple. It is no more difficult to buy or sell gold futures contracts than to buy or sell securities.

Once a trader has taken a position in the market by buying or selling one or more contracts, he has two options: either (1) maintain the position until the contract matures and then accept or make delivery, or (2) offset the contract before maturity by assuming a position equal and opposite to the original trade. In other words, if a trader originally bought one gold contract, he could liquidate or offset by selling that contract; if he originally sold a contract, he could offset by buying it back. In both cases his liquidating trade must be made for the same delivery month and on the same exchange as the original contract. Approximately 97 percent of all commitments are offset in this manner, rather than by delivery.

Market Participants—
Hedgers and Speculators

Participants in the gold futures market may be classified into two general groups—hedgers and speculators. Although the trading patterns of these groups may overlap, their motivations for participation in the market are distinctly different.

Hedgers use the market principally as a marketing and price-protection tool for establishing the price at which they will buy or sell their inventory of gold at a future date. A hedger, then, is someone involved in the physical production, processing, handling, or marketing of the actual commodity, gold in this instance. He uses the gold futures market as a financial management tool. Proper use of the market can assist him in stabilizing income, freeing working capital, reducing procurement costs, reducing inventory costs, ensuring contract obligations, and providing flexibility in timing of purchases and sales. Hedgers in the gold market might include miners, smelters, gold depositories, gold fabricators, and industrial users of fabricated gold.

The speculator's concern is with price changes only. He is motivated by the potential profit-making opportunity afforded him. He uses his risk capital in an attempt to take advantage of favorable price fluctuations in the market by buying futures when he thinks they will go up in price and selling when he believes they will go down in price. His participation in the market provides the liquidity that affords trading opportunities for hedgers at low cost.

He does not own or handle the physical commodity. He buys a contract in the hope that prices will go up, or he sells a contract in the hope that prices will go down.

Both the hedger and the speculator are essential to each other and to the successful functioning of a liquid futures market. If the futures market provided no economic function for the hedger, there would be less need for it to exist, and without the speculator to assume the hedger's risk, there would be no market. Together, they provide the needed liquidity to facilitate entry into and egress from the market.

FACTORS THAT DETERMINE
GOLD PRICES

Prices and price fluctuations of gold on the "free"-world market are not the result of chance, but are determined by powerful economic and psychological forces that continuously change. In order to predict price trends effectively, these forces must be analyzed and evaluated continually. As is true with any other commodity, the primary factors influencing gold prices are supply and demand. Supplies are obtained from production of new gold or from private or official stockpiles. The aggregate consumption of gold reflects demand.

Supply

Gold Production

More than one half of the world's yearly production of gold comes from the Republic of South Africa. Gold in South Africa tends to be found in thin seams, one to two miles or even more beneath the surface. This has meant that gold mining in South Africa has had to surmount significant technological obstacles and has had to be highly capitalized. To start a new mine in the 1890s cost about $2 million, but to start one in the 1970s cost closer to $200 million. In a recent year nearly 90 million tons of rock were extracted from the forty-six South African mines, ground or "milled" to a fine powder, and passed through a cyanide solution to yield just under 1,000 tons of gold. That amount, however, was 74 percent of the noncommunist world's production for the year. Indeed, South Africa's share of production has grown so mightily and rapidly that it is now estimated that more than one third of all the gold ever mined has come from South Africa.

It is predominantly in South Africa that a basic characteristic of the world's major gold-mining operation can be observed—in operation. Through the Chamber of Mines of South Africa, established in 1889, the seven large gold finance houses control South African gold production, refining, and marketing. Following the dictates of the Chamber of Mines, South African gold production is sold through the South African Reserve Bank.

The Chamber of Mines is trying to conserve South African gold resources. The impact of its conservation program on supply has been to promote the exploitation of lower-grade ore. Accordingly, South Africa's gold production has been 713 tons in 1976, 700 tons in 1977, 706 tons in 1978, 705 tons in 1979, 676 tons in 1980, and 658 tons in 1981.

The Soviet Union is in all likelihood the second-largest gold producer. United States Bureau of Mines figures suggest that Soviet gold production climbed from 50 million troy ounces in 1972 to 100 million in 1976. The U.S.S.R. has reportedly made strenuous efforts to increase production by lengthening the mining season, introducing more, larger, and improved equipment, and adding to the number of workers involved. But geologists were reportedly unable to maintain reserves of placer gold. The failure of exploration to keep pace with production may indicate that production of alluvial gold in Russia is reaching its peak. However, new sources were exploited successfully so that in 1981 the Soviets produced 300 tons of gold.

In addition to satisfying needs for foreign exchange arising from such problems as poor harvests, there has developed a tendency for the Soviet Union to expand free-world gold sales when gold prices are high and stop them when prices are low.

Canada and the United States, like South Africa, have experienced a production lag. However, in these North American countries much of the gold mined is a by-product or coproduct of other metals, which are not necessarily responsive to gold price changes. Canadian production has been hampered by a decline in high-grade ores, and it is possible that its long-term yields may fall significantly. Canada produced 51 tons of gold in 1980 and 50 tons in 1981 which is in line with Canada's historical averages. The United States produces approximately 40 tons of gold each year.

In summary, the wise gold analyst will watch carefully trends in gold production in South Africa and gold-selling policies pursued by the South African Reserve Bank and the Soviet Union.

Gold Stocks

The near indestructibility of gold means that the vast majority of all the metal ever mined is still in existence. Some is held in jewelry, coins, and medals, some is in industrial use and equipment, some is hoarded, and some is in government hands.

Total gold supply to the free market increased to a significant 1,448 metric tons in 1976 from 1,121 tons the previous year. The 1976 figure was the highest since the 2,649 of 1967 and the 1,836 of 1968, which were the most ever absorbed by the market.

Contributing to this increased supply were very heavy sales in 1976 by the Communist bloc (about 412 tons as compared with only 149 tons in 1975), as well as sales of investment holdings by China and substantial sales of such official stocks as those of the IMF. Meanwhile, about 966 tons of gold were mined in noncommunist countries in 1976, about equal to the 1975 total, indicating at least a temporary halt to the steep slide in gold supplies from this source that began in 1970. Gold produced as a by-product again accounted for about 10 percent of total free-world production, with Papua New Guinea realizing all of its gold output, 20.2 tons, from copper mining. The United States, Canada, and the Philippines were other significant sources of by-product gold. In 1980 total gold supply was 1,267 tons and in 1981 it was 1,182 tons.

The monthly auctions by the IMF, which began in June 1976, removed 25 million ounces from its gold reserve when it concluded its program in May of 1980. No future IMF auctions are contemplated.

Hoarding of gold is common in many countries. These holdings and the reserve assets of government testify to the centuries-old use of gold as the ultimate standard of value in times of turbulence, depression, inflation, and unrest.

Private investment in gold falls into two major categories: paper transactions, which are largely confined to the futures markets and to gold mine securities; and the physical ownership of the noble metal. One of these is the holding of small bars, particularly in Asia, the Middle East, and the Far East; the other is the purchase of bullion, again for investment or speculative purposes, which is common in European countries. The latter is difficult to track because it may be held in metal accounts, with banks, or with dealers. An estimate is usually arrived at by taking the remainder of identified flows of gold subtracted from available supplies.

Poor crop yields with the resultant reduction in farm income, and an increased demand for foreign exchange to pay for imports, led to some dishoarding in 1972; and high gold prices in 1974, in anticipation of legalized ownership of gold in the United States, led to more. When prices wavered in 1975, there was little net activity, but declining prices in the first three quarters of 1976, along with uncertainty about the price impact of the initial IMF auctions, led to considerable dishoarding. A strong rush to gold developed at the end of the year, however, with sharply rising prices, and the net twelve-month gain was estimated at a substantial 175 tons. Gold reached new highs in 1980 but the advent of high interest rates in 1980, 1981, and 1982 has kept the price of gold below $400 per ounce.

Vastly increased oil revenues in the Arab states have resulted in their increased gold purchases, and their activity shows signs of becoming a key factor in gold price movements.

Estimating Gold Supply

The supply of gold coming into the free market has ranged from a low of 1,035 metric tons in 1970 to a high of 1,448 tons in 1976. The second-highest total in the 1970s was 1,402 tons in 1973, a period of some of the most rapidly escalating gold prices in history. Clearly, world production of gold responds only slowly to increased prices. The immediate response to higher gold prices is to mine lower-grade ore, which tends to lower total gold development, and technological hurdles in gold extraction imply that producers must be assured long-term price strength before new mines will be developed. In 1982 approximately 1,000 tons of gold came into the free market.

Increased supply in the short term will come from released reserves, IMF auction sales, and dishoarding. Gold prices in the post-1972 range have been at historic highs, and even the August 1976 floor of $103 an ounce was far above the $70 of 1972, which topped previous prices. The fluctuation from $70 to a high near $200 in 1974, back down to $103 in 1976, and up again close to $170 in 1977 saw the supply to the free market relatively steady, as mentioned. But the totals used for fabrication dropped sharply from 1,390 tons in 1972 to 731 in 1974 before rebounding to 1,359 in 1976, with most of the recovery coming from carat-jewelry fabrication. These figures would indicate that demand is greatly influenced by monetary and emotional considerations, with fear of inflation being the great motivator. When fears of inflation subsided, however, in 1981 and 1982, the price of gold hovered around $350 per ounce.

Demand

There are two categories of demand for gold: (1) for bullion used for hoarding and investment and (2) for fabricated products taking a wide variety of forms. For the latter, there are gray areas, such as jewelry, which, in some cases, is bought more for investment than decoration.

Fabricator Demand

Although not at record levels in any category, commercial and industrial use of gold rose in 1976 from 1975 and continued to increase into early 1977 in carat jewelry, electronics, dentistry, and other industrial and decorative uses and in medals, medallions, and fake coins, while continuing a two-year decline in official coinage. In 1980 706 tons of fabricated gold were consumed in developed countries and 241 tons were used by developing countries. In 1981 760 tons of fabricated gold were consumed in developed countries and 432 tons in developing countries.

JEWELRY.   A good deal of the stronger demand pull came from the Middle East, where 256 metric tons of gold were used in jewelry manufactured in 1976, compared with 104 tons in 1975. Most of the demand came from the oil-rich nations and Turkey, which alone used 101 tons, thanks to record harvests, continuing currency weakness, and general economic unrest. Much of Europe's 345 tons of jewelry, up from 212 tons in 1975, was exported to the Middle East, and additional amounts went to the United States. Jewelry fabrication was also significant in North America, with 79 tons used in 1976. The Far East (including Japan) used 128 tons, the Indian subcontinent 53 tons, and Africa 48 tons. All of these global areas reported increases that have persisted for three or four years. In 1980 309 tons of fabricated gold were consumed in carat jewelry in developed countries and 209 tons in developing countries. In 1981 these numbers were 388 tons and 361 tons respectively.

ELECTRONICS.   Following a high for the 1970s of 127 metric tons of gold used in electronic products in 1973, two years of decline followed as gold prices soared. But this brief trend was reversed with a major increase to 72 tons in 1976 from 64 tons in 1975.

Most of the major electronics-producing nations increased their use of gold somewhat in 1976. Japan's rose by 4 tons to 23 tons, enabling it to move ahead of the United States, the perennial leader, which used 22 tons.

It appeared in 1977 that the hurried search for gold substitutes and more efficient use of gold in electronics, sparked by the steep rise in gold prices in 1972–74, had lost its thrust as manufacturers became accustomed to the higher price level. Future use, therefore, appeared likely to reflect general production trends. In 1980 84 tons of fabricated gold were consumed in electronics in developed countries and 2 tons in developing countries. These levels of consumption were essentially unchanged in 1981 and in 1982.

DENTISTRY.   Gold used in dentistry amounted to 70 metric tons in 1976, a new high for the seventies, up sharply from 64 tons in 1975. The increase and total use were dominated by the United States (20 tons), West Germany (15 tons), and Japan (13 tons), the historical leaders, with Germany and Japan increasing their use year to year by 3 tons each and the United States by 1.5 tons.

Most of the rise was credited to greater affluence, but some to relaxed national health insurance plans that permit a larger percentage of gold content in dental alloys than before. Some of the increase was credited to stockbuilding in anticipation of this increased use when prices were relatively low in 1976. Little change was anticipated in the use of dental gold in the immediate future. In 1980 60 tons of fabricated gold were used in dentistry in developed countries and 2 tons in developing countries. The same situation prevailed in 1981 and 1982.

OTHER INDUSTRIAL AND DECORATIVE USES.   Gold fabrication for industrial and decorative uses remains relatively stable, varying upward or downward with economic expansion or recession. It increased about 5 metric tons to 61 in 1976, the third successive "up" year, after declining slightly for three years.

The United States used more than 27 tons to account for 44 percent of the 1976 total. Major items in this section include gold-filled (rolled gold) products, liquid gold used for decorative purposes, medical and laboratory equipment, salts for electroplating in addition to those used by the electronics industry, and a variety of other, lesser uses. Only modest increases in this category are anticipated. In 1980 other industrial/decorative uses amounted to 66 tons in the developed countries and 4 tons in the developing countries. This scenario was repeated in 1981 and again in 1982.

OFFICIAL COINS.   A substantial portion of new gold supplies is used in official coinage, particularly in recent years, with 285 metric tons used in 1974, 244 in 1975, and 178 in 1976, compared with 46 to 62 in the prior four years.

Mining of Krugerrands by South Africa accounted for almost all of that nation's use of gold in coins in recent years—100 tons in 1974, 174 in 1975, and 91 in 1976—and South Africa led all other nations in such activity. Production was reduced in 1976, but sales of more than 3 million of the one-ounce coins exceeded prior years by a good margin. Heavy promotion of the Krugerrand generated continued substantial sales in 1977.

United Kingdom production of the sovereign was curtailed sharply in 1976, but most other major coin-issuing nations showed increases. Austria used more than 28 tons of gold, of which some 20 tons went into a special issue of a 1,000-schilling coin and the rest into normal production of ducats and kronen. Mexico and Turkey used more than 14 tons of gold in coinage, and Canada, mostly because of the issuance of 1 million Olympic Games coins in two denominations, used 11 tons. In 1980 fabricated gold in official coins totalled 169 tons in developed countries and 21 tons in developing countries. In 1981, 151 tons were consumed in developed countries and 50 tons in developing countries. 1982 results were comparable to 1981.

MEDALS, MEDALLIONS, AND FAKE COINS.   A so-called fake coin usually had gold content comparable to that in genuine coins, but its legitimacy is questionable. Gold used in these coins, medals, and medallions rose to more than 41 metric tons in 1976, as against 18 tons in 1975, with oil-rich Kuwait (16 tons), Iran (5 tons), and Saudi Arabia (4 tons) among the leaders. Many of the facsimile coins are made into jewelry, such as bracelets. Future demand in this classification appears to be geared to the performance of gold as an investment and its continuing popularity as a form of decoration. In 1980 18 tons were consumed in developed countries and 3 tons in developing countries. This consumption pattern was repeated in 1981 and again in 1982.

Estimating Gold Demand

Numerous factors will undoubtedly influence the total demand picture for gold. Substitutions of other metals, if less expensive, will be attempted in some areas if consumer resistance to higher gold prices is widespread. War or the threat of war always increases gold demand. But these factors aside, gold demand should fundamentally reflect the monetary situation. Thus, wide fluctuations in foreign exchange rates and unstable financial institutions may engender further distrust of paper currencies. Uncontrolled, and perhaps uncontrollable, inflation, fed by higher oil prices and growing balance of payments deficits, would continue to be reflected in demand for gold. Conversely, improvements in the monetary situation should result in reduced demand pressure for gold.

Means of attempting to measure demand for gold are necessarily general rather than precise because of the possible impact of investment, speculative, and hoarding demand. One of the measures that has been used is to emphasize gold's countercyclical tendency. Advocates of this approach compare gold trends to, particularly, stock market trends in order to emphasize inverse relations between the two. The rationale for this "indicator" of gold-demand action rests upon gold being the ultimate hedge, with demand being highest in recessions, depressions, and growing inflation, and lessening in more prosperous times.

Another "indicator" approach for measuring gold demand is to treat general commodity price trends as indicators of gold-demand trends. Thus, a significant upturn in commodity markets can be regarded as stimulating fears of inflation and so pushing gold demand.

Prior to the advent of massive speculative, investment, and hoarding demand in 1973, gold demand showed some seasonal characteristics. Moderate rises would generally occur in January and February; small corrections lasting into April would be followed by further gains in May, then by some correction in June, erasing from one third to one half of the total January-through-May move. In the second half of the year there would often be an upthrust, with yearly high prices being recorded in late August and early September. The annual September meeting of the International Monetary Fund would generally be the signal for a period of declining demand, with yearly low prices generally being recorded in December.

Hedging in Gold Futures

Speculators, as mentioned, invest in the market hoping to correctly anticipate and take advantage of price swings. Hedging, on the other hand, involves use of the futures market to protect the producer, processor, or handler of a commodity against adverse price movements that might affect his merchandising profit. How does this work in actual practice?

Hedging Examples

The following two examples will help to illustrate hedging procedure, although it should be borne in mind that in actual situations hedges may not work out as well as these, and the decision-making will not be as simple as that found in these examples.

EXAMPLE 1: MINING SMELTING COMPANY. Place Short Hedge Against Declining Prices.

The operator of Old Stakeout Mine & Smelting Company, encouraged by the upward trend in gold prices, decided to sink new shafts to tap low-grade ore existing below previously exploited veins.

It is September and gold prices have been fluctuating in recent months. There are indications of weakness in gold prices, and the management feels that prices the following summer may be considerably lower than the $180 a troy ounce currently being paid for refined gold.

The company normally experiences its heaviest sales during the summer months. Seventy-five percent of yearly production is sold in July and August. Old Stakeout management feels that $160 an ounce would assure it of a reasonable profit after considering all costs. Accordingly, a sale of June futures is undertaken at that price.

Now assume it's June and prices have in fact declined. Old Stakeout sells its inventory on the cash market at $150 an ounce and simultaneously buys back its June futures contracts at $151 an ounce. The transaction would look something like this:

Cash Market		Futures Market	
Sept. 1			
Anticipated sale price	$160/oz.	Sold June gold @	$160/oz.
June 1			
Sold gold @	$150/oz.	Bought (offset) gold @	$151/oz.
Profit from futures	$ 9/oz.	Profit from futures	$ 9/oz.
REALIZED PRICE	$159/oz.		

Old Stakeout turned a profit of $9 an ounce in the futures market and thus has sold its inventory at $159 net, $9 more than it would have received had it not hedged.

Had prices increased rather than declined during the time of the operator's hedge, his loss on the futures transaction would have been offset by his gain in cash sales. Of course, in the case of rising prices, without a hedge his cash sale would have resulted in a larger profit, but Old Stakeout management does not rely on speculation in running its business. It realized that by hedging it gave up the opportunity for extra profit, but at the same time it was ensured against obtaining a dramatically lower price. Too, the futures market is flexible. If prices trended sharply upward during the time of the hedge, management could have liquidated its position by buying back its contracts, reinstating its hedge if conditions later warranted. Such decisions would want to be carefully considered, however, as they essentially place the company in the role of speculator.

EXAMPLE 2: JEWELRY FABRICATOR.   Place Long Hedge Against Rising Prices.

A jewelry fabricator's business includes, among other items, the manufacture of high school class rings. Prices must be quoted in the fall and orders taken at that time for spring ring shipments. The fabricator's gold supplier is unwilling to quote a firm delivery price for more than a few weeks in advance. Rather than purchase the actual inventory of gold in September to cover his needs for ring manufacture in March, the fabricator decides to forward-price his gold by buying March futures contract. In this way he protects himself against a rise in gold prices.

Cash Market		Futures Market	
Sept. 1			
Ordered gold for early Mar. delivery at projected price of	$155/oz.	Bought Mar. gold @	$150/oz.
Mar. 1			
Bought gold @	$165/oz.	Sold (offset) gold @	$164/oz.
Profit from futures	$ 14/oz.	Profit from futures	$ 14/oz.
REALIZED PRICE	$151/oz.		

The $14-an-ounce profit in the futures transaction more than offset the $10 increase he paid for the actual gold, thus assuring the fabricator that he could manufacture the class rings at the raw-material cost budgeted earlier and with a slightly higher profit margin.

Conclusion

By way of conclusion, it should be noted that during most of 1980 and 1981 gold was in a bear market. After reaching $850 per troy ounce on January 21, 1980, gold fell by more than 50 percent to below $400 per ounce in July of 1982.

The overall downtrend in the price of gold from January 1980 to July 1982 was a result of high interest rates.

What has caused the price of gold to rise in the past, and what would make it go up in the future?

- Concern about the erosion in the value of paper money
- Rising inflation rates, which would result in generalized upward pressures on commodity prices
- Political crises leading to armed confrontation, especially between the superpowers
- Disruption of Middle East oil supplies to the importing industrial nations

12

Speculating in Silver, Copper, and Platinum

SILVER

Silver is both a precious metal and an industrial metal. As a precious metal, it follows the path of gold. As an industrial metal, silver is used in photography, electronics, and high-technology industries.

Sources of Supply
- World production
- Recovery of silver from industrial scrap
- Conversion of coins and objects into bullion
- Imported individual holdings
- Industrial need for metals from mines producing silver as a by-product

Demand
- Industrial use of silver
- Competition from substitute metals
- Hoarding of precious metals
- Coinage and commemorative issues
- Sterling-silver applications

Silver is the most plentiful of the precious metals. Its yearly world production of approximately 225 million troy ounces is six times that of gold and forty times that of platinum. Because silver is rarely found isolated in ores, it is primarily mined as a by-product metal with copper, lead, or zinc. The demand and price factors for these metals directly affect the supply and price of raw silver.

An important secondary source of silver is the reclamation of silver and silver-bearing waste solutions, especially from the photographic industry. Other sources include both domestic and foreign holdings by governments and individuals. These secondary areas now meet over half the annual world silver demand. From time to time in the last decade, the demand for silver has exceeded the supply. In 1980 and 1981, however, silver supplies produced a net surplus, which was added to private investor holdings. The total world silver stocks, including privately held and government stocks, are now estimated at 1.3 billion.

A lesson that bears repeating: World production and consumption of silver appear to be in balance.

See Tables 8 and 9 for historical data on world silver supplies and consumption.

In 1979 silver began trading at $6.02 per ounce and ended the year at $28 per ounce. The movement into silver was propelled by the worsening energy crisis and the deterioration of the United States dollar. Other factors were the Indian government's decision to ban the export of silver as well as a reduction in silver supplied from recycling operations. The $28 price is especially remarkable when one considers that the production cost of silver is only $7 per ounce. Commodities folklore is also replete with stories of how in this period Nelson Bunker Hunt, a billionaire Texas oilman, and Arab investors purchased 23 ounces of silver in October of 1979. The Hunt group ultimately controlled 60 million ounces of silver by the time the price of silver collapsed in January of 1980. After reaching $28, silver has fallen to an average price of $8 an ounce in 1981 and $6 an ounce in 1982. In 1982 Peru, Mexico, and Canada tried to institute an OPEC-type marketing organization to maintain the price of silver at desired levels. This effort was only modestly successful. Also in 1982 the United States Department of the Interior suspended the sale of silver from the strategic stockpile. These moves helped prevent the price of silver from falling below the $4-an-ounce benchmark.

We should reiterate some trading strategy at this point. Trading in silver requires that you keep constantly aware of the changes in supply and demand in silver around the world. Silver trading should be done on an exchange where there is significant trading volume and open interest. Needless to say, you should study technical indicators which chart the price of silver over the previous twelve months. Then start to paper-trade in the next few months. After you have simulated trading for approximately three months, analyze your results and decide if you want to begin trading in earnest.

TABLE 8. World Silver Consumption

WORLD SILVER CONSUMPTION
(Million of Ounces)

1973–1979

	1979	1978	1977	1976	1975	1974	1973
Industrial Uses:							
United States	166	160	154	170	158	177	196
Japan	65	64	63	61	46	47	69
West Germany	37	26	60	51	39	60	65
Italy	33	42	34	32	29	39	42
France	21	22	21	19	21	16	14
United Kingdom	27	29	32	28	28	25	31
India	19	20	18	18	13	15	13
Other	42	41	36	43	43	32	48
Total-Industrial Uses	410	404	418	422	377	411	478
Coinage:							
United States	.1	.1	.4	1.3	2.7	1.0	.9
Canada	.3	.3	.3	8.4	10.4	8.6	1.4
France	7.7	11.1	6.9	6.7	5.2	3.6	.1
Austria	5.0	9.5	3.0	6.9	13.4	5.6	6.6
West Germany	3.7	3.6	2.6	2.9	4.3	8.8	9.5
Others	6.0	10.4	6.0	3.5	2.8	.1	10.7
Total-Coinage Usage	22.8	35.0	19.2	29.7	38.8	27.7	29.2

TABLE 9. World Silver Supplies

WORLD SILVER SUPPLIES
(Million of Ounces)

1973–1979

	1979	1978	1977	1976	1975	1974	1973
New Production	271	265	268	247	242	237	254
U.S. Treasury Stocks	—	—	—	1	3	1	1
Scrap Recovery	81	87	80	76	73	66	60
Liquidation of (Additions to) Speculative Inventories	30	14	20	(4)	(21)	33	62
Other Sources	51	68	69	132	119	100	130
Total Available Supplies	433	434	437	452	416	437	507

COPPER

Because the demand for copper is sensitive to the overall level of economic activity, any deep recession must lead to a sharp decline in copper prices. Copper prices remained depressed after the last recession (1973–75) for an unusually long period (four years), however, because of sustained increases in supply even with low prices and record-high stocks. In 1982 the early improvement in industrial production faded as most Western economies followed the United States into recession. The automotive and housing industries remained depressed. Exchange prices for copper fell to levels below costs for many mines.

Copper prices remained depressed for four years following the last recession. To assess the probable recurrence of this situation after the current recession, it will be useful to review what happened during and after the last recession.

1974–79

Copper prices on the LME fell 62 percent from peak to trough in the last recession, from an average of 137 cents a pound in April 1974 to 52 cents in December 1975. From 1975 to 1978 they averaged 56 to 64 cents. The depressed state of the copper industry during this period was basically the result of demand/supply imbalances. Data for free-world copper production, consumption, stocks, and prices on the LME from 1974 to 1979 follow.

Free World Refined Copper

| Year | (THOUSANDS OF METRIC TONS) | | | |
	Production	Consumption	Stocks	LME Prices (cent/lb.)
1974	6945	6495	713	93
1975	6264	5440	1357	56
1976	6641	6643	1443	64
1977	6875	6887	1508	59
1978	6913	7289	1185	62
1979	7030	7412	731	90

Copper demand is closely tied to economic activity and is therefore greatly influenced by fluctuations in the business cycle. In 1975, when the level of economic activity in most industrialized countries either declined or slowed, free-world consumption of copper fell sharply. Copper production also fell, but the decline was not large enough to offset the decrease in consumption. The excess of output over usage resulted in a buildup of stocks. In 1976, despite low prices and rising stocks, free-world copper production increased by 6 percent. The continued increases in production in face of excessive stocks resulted in large part because several important copper-producing developing countries needed foreign exchange to service heavy external debt obligations, which arose to a significant extent because of sharp increases in oil prices. In addition, copper output also rose in industrialized nations, since producers did not anticipate the continued buildup in stocks.

As examples, in 1976 Chile increased its mine production of copper by 21 percent from the previous year, while the increase in the United States was 14 percent. In 1977 mine production rose 46 percent in Peru and 12 percent in Zaire. The growth in world copper production combined with low levels of consumption resulted in a huge accumulation of stocks in 1976 and 1977. World copper stocks rose to 1.5 million metric tons in 1977 versus 713,000 in 1974. Stocks on the LME warehouses rose from about 130,000 metric tons to around 640,000 in 1977. This unprecedented buildup in stocks kept copper prices depressed.

In 1978 and 1979 numerous events occurred that caused a continuous drawdown of stocks. The level of free-world copper consumption improved, as copper demand in the United States, Japan, and in most West European countries rose in both years. As for supply, free-world mine production fell by 4 percent in 1978 and remained almost flat in 1979. Contributing factors included industry strikes in Canada, political turmoil and transport problems in Zaire and Zambia, and closure of a number of mines for various reasons, one of which was depressed prices. By the end of 1979, world copper stocks had fallen significantly, from 1.5 million metric tons in 1977 to 731,000 tons. Stocks on the LME warehouses fell from 640,000 to 125,000 tons. Copper prices on the LME averaged 90 cents in 1979 versus 62 in 1978. By year end 1979, the price of copper was about $1.00 a pound, a third higher than at the beginning of the year.

January–June 1980

With copper stocks at the beginning of 1980, copper prices were poised for sharp increases early in the year—at least until clear signs of recession appeared. Two additional factors, however, led to truly dramatic increases in copper prices. First, unexpectedly high inflation rates in the United States and several other major industrialized countries in early 1980 spurred investor interest in tangible assets, such as commodities. Second—but most important—developments in Iran and Afghanistan (as well as controversial dealings in the silver market) fueled the demand for precious metals, and copper (as poor man's gold) was carried along with the surge in gold and silver prices. In addition, copper is particularly sensitive to threats of war because of its widespread use in many forms of ordnance.

The price of both gold and silver peaked on January 21, 1980, but the upward momentum in copper prices (referred to fondly by traders as the "Ayatollah rally") was sustained until mid-February, when copper hit 143.7 cents a pound on the LME. Then, the combination of record-high interest rates, an emerging recession in the United States, and declining gold and silver prices began to deflate the copper bubble. Copper prices fell to 105 cents a pound in March 1980, and by the end of

April declined to 90 cents a pound, reaching an unheard-of low of 52 cents a pound in June of 1982.

How the Current Recession Compares with the 1973–75 Recession

Similarities

1. In the last recession copper prices on the LME fell 62 percent from peak to trough in a period of eight months. In the current recession copper prices have already fallen significantly, by about 30 percent from their peak in February to the end of April, a period of three months, but they have since stabilized. Destabilization set in early in 1980 and continued through 1982 with LME copper quoted below the cost of production.

2. World copper stocks are about the same at the beginning of the current recession as at the beginning of the last recession.

3. The construction industry, which accounts for 25 percent of the American copper market, is in a slump. Housing starts in the United States have shown declines comparable to the past recession, while commercial construction has weakened considerably in 1981 and 1982 as a result of unavailability of mortgage financing.

4. The transportation sector, which in normal times absorbs about 15 percent of total United States copper consumption, is quite depressed. Auto sales in the United States are as bad now as they were in the past recession. In 1982 new car sales fell to unprecedented levels, resulting in the near bankruptcy of Chrysler Corporation and staggering layoffs at both General Motors and Ford.

5. A significant weakness in retail sales in the United States has developed.

6. Copper-producing developing countries are still having problems servicing their debts. Zambia is currently in arrears with its foreign exchange payments. About $2 billion of Zaire's external debt, which matured in 1979, had to be rescheduled. Zambia and Zaire, to earn precious foreign exchange for the importation of oil, continue to produce copper and sell it on an extremely depressed world market.

Differences

1. Interest rates have dropped from recent highs more quickly in this cycle, indicating that the current recession will probably be shorter than the last one. Housing starts in particular will recover earlier than in the last recession.

2. Real defense spending in the United States rose 2 percent in 1982.

In the last recession real defense spending in the United States fell 5.2 percent from the fourth quarter of 1973 to the first quarter of 1975 and remained essentially flat for several years thereafter. Copper is sometimes referred to as the "war metal." In 1982 30,000 tons of copper were consumed by the military.

3. The economies of other industrialized countries were somewhat out of phase with the U.S. economy, minimizing the possibility of a world recession. However, most Western economies followed the United States into recession in 1981–1982.

4. The recent period seems to have been largely free of the hoarding of copper and other raw materials that occurred prior to the last recession.

5. The 1980 strike in the copper industry reduced output by 400,000 tons. In contrast, the brief strike in 1977 hardly affected output. In this context, the strike should have been bullish for copper prices, offsetting some of the bearish influences of the recession. It wasn't because Canadian, Australian, and Chilean producers picked up the slack.

Copper Price Forecast: Most Optimistic Case

If we forecast that real GNP in the United States will decline about 3 percent in this recession from peak to trough, as opposed to a decline of 5.7 percent during the last recession, we expect copper prices to continue falling during the second half of 1982 and to remain relatively low for a period thereafter. The percentage decline, however, will most likely not be as great as during the last recession, and the period of depressed prices will probably be significantly shorter than after the last recession.

Aside from the the factors influencing the demand for copper, an important consideration in this guardedly optimistic forecast is the inability of producers to expand supply as after the last recession. This point will be explored further in the next section (the worst case forecast).

Based on these supply and demand factors, copper prices averaged about 96 cents a pound in 1980, compared to 90 cents in 1979. We expect copper prices to decline during the second half of 1982 and in 1983—conceivably to as low as 50 cents—for two reasons.

1. The effect of recession operates on copper demand with a delay, and the continuing lagged effect of recession in the United States will lead to a contraction in U.S. demand for copper.

2. Demand for copper outside the United States is likely to become sluggish as real growth slows in other countries.

It should be recognized that at times copper prices can be quite sensitive to developments in the precious metals markets. The current stability in copper prices is partly the result of the most recent upturn in gold prices. In a rather perverse manner, political stress worldwide will lend support to copper prices, while resolution of conflicts is decidely bearish for the copper market.

Copper Price Forecast: Worst Case

By assumption, demand in this case falls roughly in proportion to the last recession. Such a decline would certainly lead to a plunge in prices; a significant decline is already evident. The problem was compounded in the last recession and in the years thereafter, however, by sustained increases in supply even with excessive stocks and depressed prices. The real question regarding the price outlook in this case, then, concerns the supply response.

In the period after the last recession, developing countries heavily dependent on copper for foreign exchange maintained high levels of production to service their external debts, even though the increases in supply kept copper prices depressed. The same debt problems remain today in many cases. Moreover, the continuous increasing of oil prices has once again created balance of payments problems for these countries. The problem of buying oil in the spot market because of the cutoff of Iranian oil has also added to whatever difficulties they may have already had in servicing their debts. To acquire foreign exchange, they may very well try to maintain, as before, a high level of copper production regardless of price and the fact that stocks will be rising.

Political instability among major copper-producing developing countries, however, could result in an interruption of copper production in some countries. For example, mine production of copper in Zaire, the fifth largest producer of copper, has never fully recovered from the invasion of Shaba province in May 1978. Mine production of copper has fallen from 500,000 metric tons in 1974 to about 385,000 in 1979. Zaire's foreign exchange problems have been such that they have not been able to obtain needed spare parts for the maintenance of mining equipment. However, Zaire managed to produce 456,000 tons in 1980, 467,000 in 1981, and 480,000 in 1982.

Zambia, the fourth largest producer of copper, is also in political turmoil and has been plagued by transportation problems. Copper output has fallen from 780,000 metric tons in 1976 to about 580,000 in 1979. Zambia has apparently lost some of its vital technical people; this could have negative long-run effects on its copper production. Again, Zambia produced 617,000 tons in 1980, 631,000 tons in 1981, and 642,000 tons in 1982. Zimbabwe remains relatively free of political turmoil following its independence. Zambia, however, may resume exporting through Zimbabwe, which would help alleviate Zambia's transportation problem.

Based on a September 1979 survey by Phelps Dodge, limited capacity additions worldwide are projected through 1983, and no major new mines except possibly Iran's Sar Chesmeh—an unlikely occurrence—are expected to come on stream by 1983. The huge Codelco mine in Chile is considered to have reached its peak producing years and is expected to experience erosion of output in the coming years. These expected shortfalls in production will keep copper prices from falling to levels as low as in the past recession.

On the demand side, copper consumption in the free world rose by 11 percent from 1974 to 1978, while in developing countries growth was 31 percent. With their high growth rates, a number of developing countries can quickly join the ranks of significant consumers. By the mid-1980s, as demand consistently outweighs new production, a true shortage of supply will likely develop along with sharp increases in copper prices.

The fundamental conclusion of our analysis is that in any conceivable circumstances copper prices will neither fall as low nor remain as depressed for as long as after the last recession.

A typical brokerage house statement of 177 short copper contracts is shown in Figure 3.

STATEMENT OF ACCOUNT — OPEN TRADES

APR 30 · 1982

ACCOUNT NUMBER
002 09110

NON—REGULATED COMMODITIES

*GRAINS IN 000S

E.&O.E.

DATE	POSITION* LONG	POSITION* SHORT	COMMODITY	TRADE PRICE	OPEN TRADE EQUITY DEBIT	OPEN TRADE EQUITY CREDIT
2/16/82		1	MAY 82 COPPER	73.65		737.50
2/16/82		1	MAY 82 COPPER	73.75		762.50
2/17/82		2	MAY 82 COPPER	73.75		1,525.00
2/17/82		1	MAY 82 COPPER	73.80		775.00
2/18/82		1	MAY 82 COPPER	73.45		687.50
2/19/82		2	MAY 82 COPPER	74.00		1,650.00
2/19/82		2	MAY 82 COPPER	74.05		1,675.00
2/19/82		2	MAY 82 COPPER	74.25		1,775.00
2/19/82		3	MAY 82 COPPER	74.30		2,700.00
2/19/82		2	MAY 82 COPPER	74.35		1,825.00
2/19/82		3	MAY 82 COPPER	74.55		2,887.50
2/23/82		21	MAY 82 COPPER	72.60		9,975.00
2/23/82		3	MAY 82 COPPER	72.75		1,537.50
2/23/82		10	MAY 82 COPPER	72.80		5,250.00
2/24/82		41	MAY 82 COPPER	71.90		12,300.00
2/24/82		7	MAY 82 COPPER	71.95		2,187.50
	*	102*	SETTLEMENT PRICE	70.70		48,250.00*
2/23/82		7	JUL 82 COPPER	75.10		4,725.00
2/25/82		5	JUL 82 COPPER	74.05		2,062.50

DATA PROCESSING BY COMPUTER INFORMATION SERVICE, INC.

RETAIN FOR TAX RECORDS

FIGURE 3. Copper Short Sale

PLATINUM

Platinum is known as a metal with great resistance to attack. Its many uses in industry derived from its ability to withstand high temperatures, acid damage, disintegrating atmospheres, and great stress. In 1981 United States platinum purchases showed:

Use	Percent of Total
Automotive	57.0
Petroleum	12.1
Electrical	8.2
Chemical	7.0
Glass	6.3
Jewelry and decorative	2.0
Dental and medical	1.9
All other	5.5

The American automotive industry emerged in 1974 as the largest single major outlet for platinum. The use of platinum is concentrated in the emission controls area. In 1981 purchases of platinum by the industry for stockpiling and consumption equaled 805,000 ounces, accounting for most of total United States purchases. In both the petroleum and chemical industries platinum is used principally as a catalyst. Platinum plays a critical catalytic role in the manufacture of gasoline and of nitric acid, an intermediate for fertilizers, explosives, and plastics. Electrical and electronic uses of platinum include temperature measuring devices and circuit elements. The glass industries consume platinum in the manufacture of fiberglass. Gem settings constitute the single most important jewelry use.

In the supply side a substantial portion of the total U.S. supply is accounted for by recycling. The rest is imported from South Africa, Canada, and the Soviet Union. South Africa produces platinum as a primary product. Canadian production is associated with the nickel industry where platinum is primarily a by-product of palladium.

1981 Total Platinum Production

South Africa	68%
U.S.S.R.	28%
Canada	3%
All other	1%

Speculating in Platinum

Purchasing the Contract: February 1

An investor, after careful study of recent platinum consumption and production trends, concludes that platinum futures are undervalued over the period of the next six months. The current price for a July futures contract of the same year is $325 per ounce. The investor purchases five contracts at this price, with a total value of $81,250.

Selling the Contract: June 25

On June 25 the price of the July contract has risen to $355 per

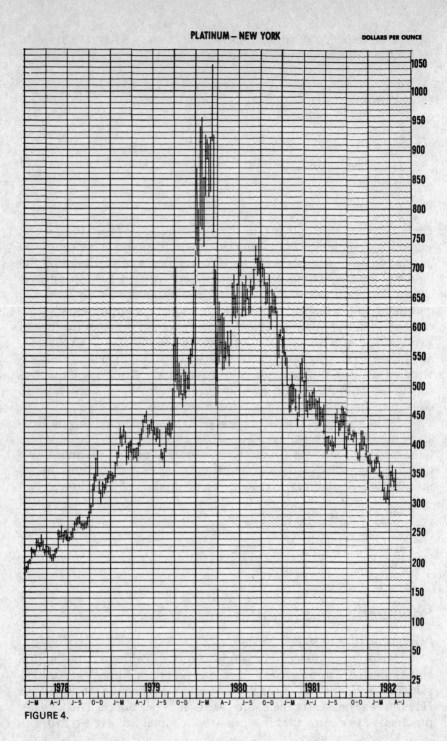

PLATINUM – NEW YORK

DOLLARS PER OUNCE

FIGURE 4.

ounce. The investor concludes, based upon an analysis of all conditions, that it is desirable to sell at this level. He sells his five contracts, representing a total value of sale of $88,750. He has realized a profit of $7,500, less his round turn commission charges.

The above example was based upon the conclusion by the investor that a rise in the platinum market was to be anticipated.

A Final Caveat About Platinum

This is a precious metal whose fortunes are tied to the U.S. automotive industry. If Americans are not buying new cars, then platinum will usually be trading at its historic lows.

13

Speculating in Strategic Metals

A discussion of metals would not be complete without looking at the so-called minor, or "strategic," metals. They are essential because they provide the metallurgical base for the industrial world; they are strategic because they occur in nature in the third world, the Soviet Union, and in potentially unstable countries such as South Africa.

A speculator in strategic metals runs even greater risk than his platinum counterpart because strategic metals are not traded on a commodity exchange. What you are asked to do is to purchase, for example, one kilogram of germanium for $1,000 and to sit with this investment for three to five years in the hope that the price of germanium will double or even triple in that time. Meanwhile, your money is not earning any interest. No leverage is involved because you have paid 100 percent of the purchase price.

Still interested? Then here are some of the more "strategic" of the strategic metals (1981 production figures).

Metal	Use	Production	Projected Demand
Antimony	Increasing use in flame-retardant formulations for plastics, textiles, and rubber; decreasing use as hardener in lead storage batteries.	*World production:* 79,000 short tons. *U.S. mine production:* 800 short tons. *U.S. consumption:* 42,000 short tons (53% of world production). *Major world producers:* South Africa (20%), China (20%), Bolivia (17%), U.S.S.R. (10%).	The depletion of high-grade ore deposits in Bolivia and Mexico likely to increase future production costs.
Bismuth	Used primarily in pharmaceuticals and chemicals, and, in the manufacture of machinery parts in the primary metal industry, in low melting point alloys.	*World production:* 9.4 million pounds. *U.S. mine production:* low (unreported). *U.S. consumption:* 2.5 million pounds (26% of world production). *Major world producers:* Australia (22%), Mexico (16%), Peru (15%), Bolivia (11%), Soviet bloc (11%).	World demand expected to increase through 1990; U.S. reliance on imported bismuth expected to continue.
Cadmium	Used in the electroplating industry for plated hardware, in nickel-cadmium batteries, stabilizers for vinyl plastics and pigments.	*World production:* 18,280 metric tons. *U.S. mine production:* 1,700 metric tons. *U.S. consumption:* 4,800 metric tons (27% of world production). *Major world producers:* Soviet bloc (23%), Japan (14%), U.S. (9%), Canada (8%), Belgium (8%). (Cadmium is produced as a by-product of zinc.)	U.S. demand for cadmium is expected to increase at an annual rate of about 1.8% through 1990.
Germanium	The instrumental and optical industries are primary consumers. Germanium is also used in a variety of electronic and electrical applications and in the production of certain military hardware.	*World production:* 109,000 kilograms. *U.S. production:* 27,000 kilograms. *U.S. consumption:* 35,000 kilograms. *Major world producers:* U.S. (21%). Soviet bloc (8%). (Germanium is a by-product of certain domestic zinc ores.)	Many special uses in a wide variety of industries, with tremendous growth potential in these areas. U.S. demand is expected to increase at an annual rate of 5% through 1990.

Metal	Use	Production	Projected Demand
Indium	Used in plating electrical and electronic components, solders, alloys, and coatings, and in nuclear reactor control rods.	*World production:* 1.5 million troy ounces. *Major world producers:* Soviet bloc (22%), Japan (13.3%), Canada (10%), Peru (6.6%). (Occurs primarily in zinc sulfide ores.) *U.S. production:* None.	U.S. consumption increasing approximately 3% per annum. Additional uses developing in dental alloys, jewelry, optics, and compounds used in infrared devices.
Iridium	Platinum alloy for high-temperature crucibles and compass bearings.	*World production:* Total for platinum-group metals, 6.7 million troy ounces. *U.S. production:* None. *U.S. consumption:* 35,000 troy ounces. *Major world producers:* South Africa and U.S.S.R. (96%). (Iridium is essentially produced as a by-product of platinum and palladium.)	United States consumption increasing approximately 5% per annum.
Manganese	Regarded as a "war material" during most of this century. Essential in steel production. Each ton of carbon steel contains about twelve pounds of manganese. Also used in the production of pig iron, dry-cell batteries, and in various chemical processes.	*World production:* 27 million short tons. *U.S. production:* None. *U.S. consumption:* (1) manganese ore, 1,372,000 short tons (35%–54% manganese content); (2) ferromanganese, 976,000 short tons (74%–95% manganese content). *Major world producers:* Soviet bloc (43.5%), South Africa (20%), Australia (6.7%). (U.S.S.R. and South Africa account for 80% of world's resources.)	The market economics are completely dependent on one country, South Africa, for supplies, particularly for the higher grade ferromanganese ore. A recent study has found that eastern bloc countries have been importing increasing quantities of manganese and that this dependency is a permanent condition.
Mercury	Used in production of electrical instruments, the electrolytic preparation of chlorine and caustic soda, in industrial and control instruments and the manufacture of mildew proof.	*World production:* 190,200 flasks. *U.S. production:* 33,200 flasks (one mine producing 20,000 flasks). *U.S. consumption:* 42,000 flasks. *Major world producers:* Soviet bloc (45%), U.S. (17.5%), Algeria (16%), Spain (16%).	Growing use expected in batteries and caustic soda manufacture. Continuing low prices have kept major producing nations at a curtailed operation status. Few satisfactory substitutes.

Molybdenum (1) Metallurgical—used as an alloying agent in steels to enhance hardenability, strength, toughness, wear, and corrosion resistance. (2) As a refractory metal in the chemical industry to produce many petroleum-based products. Wide use in ornament and in transportation and aerospace systems.

World production: 227 million pounds. *U.S. production:* 143,967,000 pounds. *U.S. consumption:* 63 million pounds. *Major world producers:* U.S. (63%), Canada (14%), U.S.S.R. (10%), Chile (13%).

Bulk of world reserves are contained in relatively few large deposits with diminishing reserves. From 1975 to 1979 U.S. demand grew at an annual rate of 7.3%. Expected demand will be greater in developing and European nations. Growing use in the manufacture of low-temperature-resistant pipeline steel for use in Arctic regions. U.S. inventories have been decreasing. No acceptable substitute in numerous uses.

Rhodium Rhodium has a high resistance to corrosion and is alloyed with platinum in electrical equipment, used as a catalyst in automobiles, and in the production of nitric acid.

World production: 3,000,000 pounds. *U.S. production:* none. *U.S. consumption:* 110,000 ounces. *Major world producers:* South Africa and U.S.S.R. (96%).

Demand for use in catalytic converters in the auto industry increasing in both Japan and U.S.

Selenium Major uses in electronic and photocopier components, glass manufacture, chemicals, and pigments.

World production: 3,444,000 pounds. *U.S. production:* 587,000 pounds. *U.S. consumption:* 318,000 pounds. *Major world producers* (refineries): Canada (34%), Japan (28%), U.S. (17%). (Selenium is a by-product of the electrolytic refining of copper.)

Anticipated use in the manufacture of photovoltaic solar cells (which are used in the direct conversion of sunlight to electrical energy) may have fundamental effects on supply/demand equation.

Tellurium Used as an agent in steel and copper alloys, in the chilling of malleable cast iron, and as a curing agent and accelerator in rubber compounding. Also used as a chemical catalyst in the manufacture of glass and in a variety of photosensitive instruments.

World production: 460,000 pounds. *U.S. production:* 131,000 pounds. *U.S. consumption:* 260,000 pounds. *Major world producers* (refineries): Canada (30%), U.S. (30%).

The Department of Energy has been supporting a research program that has studied the possibility of using cadmium telluride in the manufacture of photovoltaic solar cells (used in the direct conversion of sunlight to electrical energy).

Metal	Use	Production	Projected Demand
Titanium	Has wide usage including aerospace, aircraft, petrochemical, ships, and weaponry. Is twice as strong as steel while being lightweight, corrosion-resistant, low in density, and easy to fabricate. Has no known substitutes in aircraft and aerospace uses. Obtained primarily from ilmenite and rutile.	*World production:* 110,000 short tons. *U.S. mine production:* withheld by mining companies. *U.S. consumption:* 26,943 short tons. *Major world producers:* Soviet Union (35%), China (20%), U.S. (10%), Australia (10%), Japan (5%).	1980—60% titanium metal used for jet engines, airframes, and space and missile applications. 1980 U.S. imports up 80% over 1979 and supply fell as production capacities increased 13%. From 1979 base demand expected to increase at 5% annual rate through 1990 while production is nearing capacity.
Vanadium	Used primarily as an alloying agent for iron and steel. Also used as a strengthening agent for titanium-based alloys and as a catalyst in the chemical industry.	*World production:* 83.1 million pounds. *U.S. production:* 11,517,000 pounds. *U.S. consumption:* 16 million pounds. *Major world producers:* South Africa (32%), Soviet bloc (26%), China (17%), U.S. (14%).	Future consumption should grow with increased demand for high-performance materials. It is claimed that the Soviet Union is a net importer of vanadium from Finland and indirectly from South Africa through Western European procurers. Here again, the U.S. is dependent on South African supplies.

IV

SPECULATING IN
ENERGY FUTURES

14

All Roads Lead
to Saudi Arabia

The Commodity Futures Trading Commission (CFTC) granted approval to the New York Mercantile Exchange to begin trading contracts of No. 2 heating oil in 1978. Subsequently, additional trading in these products has been launched by the International Petroleum Exchange in London. Additionally, the New York Mercantile Exchange will also offer gasoline futures.

HOW CAN I HEDGE IN PETROLEUM?

There used to be an old adage in the oil business: "You make your money on exploration and operate your marketing at break-even." This strategy worked well until:

- The Arab oil embargo in 1973
- The Iranian crisis of 1979
- Full decontrol of petroleum prices

With the creation of OPEC and other "energy shocks," the major integrated oil companies have discovered that profitability from exploration is no longer guaranteed, and all petroleum marketers will have to pay closer attention to changes in supply and demand.

As prices of petroleum products fluctuated widely in response to supply/demand fundamentals, buyers and sellers engaged in a protracted struggle to obtain fixed-price, 18-months contracts as a means of insulating themselves from wide swings in prices. Another consideration is the existence of a two-tier market—a contract market and a spot market. The contract market covers 90 percent of the product being distributed, with the spot market accounting for the balance. The petroleum spot market works like any spot market: if a supplier runs out of product from his or her contracted source he purchases it from another source at a premium.

A WORD ABOUT CONVERGENCE

As the futures contract month approaches its expiration, the futures price tends to approach or "converge" on the cash price. If there is a difference in the cash and futures price, the possibility for arbitrage exists. Earlier we looked at a "cash and carry" transaction. From that example, we saw that if the cash price is below the futures price by more than the cost of carrying the product until delivery, you would:

- Buy the Cash Product
- Sell the Futures
- Deliver the product to close out the futures contract against payment.

THE ART OF HEDGING

Let's say you're an oil distributor buying products from contractual suppliers as well as on the "spot" market. You normally build up product in the summer months that you begin to deliver in September. This brings us to the use of the "short hedge."

On May 1, let us say you buy 420,000 gallons at 95¾ cents on the spot market. This you take into inventory. Simultaneously, you hedge this inventory by selling ten September futures contracts (each contract is 42,000 gallons) at $1.0025 per gallon. Suppose the market declines 2 cents per gallon at the time you have to deliver your product at 93¾ cents per gallon. Since the cash and futures markets converge as a contract approaches expiration, the September contract was valued at $.9415 per gallon. When you liquidate your futures position, you earned $1.0610 per gallon.

Cash Market	Futures Market
April 16 buys 420,000 gallons @ $.9575	April 16 sells 10 Sept @ $1.0025
Aug 25 sells 420,000 gallons @ $.9375	Aug 25 buys 10 Sept @ $ .9415
Loss on Cash, 2¢ per gallon	Gain on futures, $.0610/gallon
Net Gain = $.0410 per gallon	

This is pretty basic stuff, but many of these principles bear repeating. Of course, there is a long hedge, too, where you need protection from rising price. Here, you may want to sign a contract with a consumer at a fixed price to be determined at delivery time. You would buy futures contracts (the "long hedge") equivalent to your delivery commitment. Come delivery time, you would purchase product in the spot market and the only loss experienced would be made up when you liquidated your long position.

In Part Two, which focused on financial futures, we discussed the "bull spread." Here we are also assuming "full carry," that the market was reflecting the full costs of storage, insurance, and prevailing interest rates. This means that the distant months were selling at a premium compared to the near by. However, if you have a long hedge in a declining market, it is conceivable that you could lose more than if you had no hedge at all.

Another trading technique is "spreading," or the simultaneous purchase and sale of different contract months. The price differences between months represent the costs of carrying product for the time between deliveries (storage, insurance, finance) as well as market expectations about the futures product prices. When futures delivery months show successive premiums, the market is said to be a carrying charge market. When the near months gain on the distant months and eventually trade at a premium to the deferred contracts, this is known as an invested market, or "backwardation." Generally, if supplies of a commodity become tight, such as in the case of an unexpected frost threatening a crop, or a severe winter cold spell late in the season in the case of number 2 heating oil, traders will bid up the front months as they seek to obtain the commodity immediately, before prices escalate. When supplies are plentiful, commodity markets will exhibit some or all of the carrying costs. The changing relationships between contract markets should be monitored closely, for they can be used to the hedger's benefit. When choosing a month to hedge, the buyer should be aware of both his or her own marketing needs and the spread differences between contract months.

Another trading technique that was previously discussed is "arbitrage," the simultaneous purchase and sale of contracts in two different physical markets. Arbitrage is similar to spreading.

Finally, the most important element to a successful hedging strategy is a thorough knowledge and familiarity with the "basis." The basis is defined as the price difference between the cash commodity at a given delivery point and the nearby or a distant future. In simple terms, the basis is the price of the cash commodity versus the futures price, or the spread between a cash and futures price. Generally, the basis value will depend upon the cost of storage, insurance, and financing charges for the cash commodity over a given period. However, locational and product differences may also be factored into a basis calculation. If a user, for example, is hedging heating oil or gasoline with a different sulfur content or octane rating than that which is specified in the contract, the price fluctuations of that particular grade may not match exactly the futures price—the basis may either narrow or widen somewhat. The principles involved in utilizing changing cash and futures relationships are similar to those the hedger would apply to changing spread relationships. For example, if a dealer holds inventory and sells futures as a hedge, he or she is "long the basis." The dealer will then profit if spot prices rise more than futures prices, or if futures prices decline more than spot oil. When the dealer is obligated to deliver product and purchases futures against his or her short inventory position, then the dealer is "short the basis." If futures advance more than spot oil prices, the distributor receives an additional profit on the futures side of the hedge.

SUMMARY

The techniques we have just reviewed reflect a much changed oil industry from even so recent a year as 1980. As Middle East oil supplies become increasingly precarious (both internally and from the Soviets), the price of all petroleum products will reflect this uncertainty. The United States oil industry will become more concentrated (witness the mad scramble for the domestic oil reserves of Marathon Oil). As our supply of both oil and natural gas from the Middle East is eventually severed, we could witness unprecedented premiums being paid for these essential commodities.

V

SPECULATING IN
TROPICAL COMMODITIES

15

Speculating in Cocoa Futures

One of the most important agricultural products of the tropics is the cocoa bean, which eventually reaches the consumer in such forms as eating or drinking chocolate, bakery products, and so on.

Legend has it that Columbus returned from America and presented King Ferdinand with cocoa beans, the source of cocoa. The Spanish aristocracy took to cocoa and, soon thereafter, cocoa was planted in Spain's overseas possessions and a thriving industry was born.

Today, major producers of cocoa are Ghana, the Ivory Coast, Cameroon, and Nigeria in Africa; and Brazil and Ecuador in South America; and Malaysia. The major consumers (in descending order) are the United States, West Germany, Brazil, the Netherlands, and the USSR.

Sharp price changes often occur, depending on the numerous developments that influence the market price. Changing crop prospects, caused by unexpected drought or other adverse weather while the crop is growing, and damage by insects and cocoa tree diseases, make it difficult to foretell the exact amount of future supplies. Sometimes, manmade barriers, such as wars, strikes, or political developments in the tropical producing areas, retard the movement of supplies to the United States and other consuming nations. Demand prospects are also subject to the vigors of changing conditions, such as trends in the business cycle that influences buying power in the consuming countries. Sometimes, high cocoa prices reduce the rate of actual consumption, while low prices may stimulate demand.

The Formation of a Cocoa Exchange

The establishment of a cocoa futures market by the cocoa industry in 1925 was a logical development. Production and consumption had been rapidly expanding since the 1900s, and cocoa was becoming one of the important commodities of world commerce. The problem of moving the crop from producing areas in the tropics to the consuming countries involved continuously greater financial risks on the part of cocoa markets. The time factor made the financing problem more difficult. Most cocoa is produced during four months of the year— October through January. For proper storage, it was necessary to move the cocoa from the tropics to temperate zones quickly. Thus, the intermediary merchants were forced to carry the crops until they were desired by the processors. It was obvious to the trade that a futures market for hedging purposes was needed. However, the industry was slow to take action until it experienced the general commodity boom and bust that followed the termination of World War I.

The Bubble Bursts

The postwar boom proved for all times the disastrous consequences of reckless speculation that occurs in commodities where there are no organized exchanges. Cocoa beans were a favorite medium of speculation for many. Speculators bought heavily and stored the cocoa beans until prices would advance. Manufacturers were forced to buy their requirements in competition with these speculators, leading to an unsuitable price increase. The crash came in 1921, as speculators unloaded inventories to pay past due bank loans. Prices plummeted drastically and many fortunes were lost. The survivors of the crash insured that this would never happen again and set about to organize a cocoa futures exchange to moderate future price movements in cocoa.

Speculating in Cocoa Futures

The standard trading unit is ten metric tons. Let's say you're a cocoa merchant and you must continually have available various grades of cocoa to meet customer requirements. Most of the season's supply becomes available with the harvests of the main crops in Africa and Brazil during the fall and early winter. Therefore, the merchant must acquire a considerable part of his or her supply at that time, and carry it until needed by processors. Without access to price insurance, the merchant would be subject to the risk of severe losses from possible declines in inventory values. When our merchant buys actual cocoa from the producing country, he immediately sells an equivalent amount of futures in the exchange. When our merchant sells his actual cocoa, he buys back a similar amount of the futures that he previously sold as a hedge. If the market has advanced and he is forced to pay more for the purchase of futures, this loss is balanced by the gain in the value of his inventory of actuals. If the price declines, his loss in inventory value is made up by the profit in buying back his futures contracts at a lower price.

16

Speculating
in Coffee Futures

The origin of coffee can be traced to ancient Abyssinia (now Ethiopia), where the coffee tree still grows, and also to Southern Arabia. Coffee seedlings spread through the Arab regions. In 1683, invading Turkish armies were stopped outside Vienna, leaving behind sacks of coffee beans. Consumption of coffee quickly spread through Europe.

Coffee trees came to the New World from France and were at first planted only in Martinique and then in Brazil. The Jesuits are credited with bringing coffee plants to Colombia. Coffee has been the most popular United States beverage since 1773.

It takes from three to five years for a new coffee tree to yield a pound of coffee. If the tree survives disease, insects, drought, flooding rains, earthquakes, and frost, it can have a lifespan of twenty to twenty-five years. Each year a typical fully groomed tree will yield enough beans to fill a 1-pound can of ground coffee on the supermarket shelf. Coffee is generally produced on small land holdings. Coffee is grown in more than fifty countries, along the earth's warmer latitudes, at altitudes from sea level to 6,000 feet. The coffee in the cup derives from two main species of seed: arabica, grown mainly in Latin America; and robusta, grown mainly in Africa.

Coffee cultivation begins with nurturing the seeds for nine to eighteen months in nurseries or in sun sheltered clusters. When the seedlings grow to about twenty-four inches, they are transplanted to permanent groves but are still protected from overexposure to sun. It takes another eighteen months to achieve white flowering. Six months later, green berries begin to bud and ripen into rich red cherries. Inside each cherry, within a reddish-yellow pulp and clothed in a silvery skin and parchment coat, are two coffee beans, newly ready for harvesting. The beans are removed from the cherries by one of two methods: (1) washed and (2) unwashed.

The beans are then bagged for transportation to the warehouse or for the exporter. The overall export coffee income of the producing regions has averaged about $14 billion a year. The United States is the largest importer of coffee.

For decades, the countries dependent on coffee exports for the revenue essential to their development suffered from the destabilizing effects of boom-and-bust cycles. The booms were short, but each triggered a new round of overproduction, which in turn led to long periods of bust because the excess coffee stocks depressed export prices.

In 1962, the governments of the major exporting and importing countries negotiated the first International Coffee Agreement in a joint attempt to prevent extreme price fluctuations in the world market. The agreement of 1962 lasted for five years and was followed by the agreements of 1968 and 1976. President Kennedy was a prime mover for the first coffee agreement. He voiced his belief that the persisting decline in coffee prices were undermining his Alliance for Progress program to assist the development of Latin America. Every succeeding President has also supported ideas leading to the coffee agreements.

Continuing with the story, the aroma and flavor of coffee are still locked within the green beans when they arrive at the points of entry. The beans are shipped to roasting houses, where they are roasted to golden brown and swell to about twice their original size. After roasting, the beans are left to cool to room temperature, then shuttled into machines that granulate the beans into grinds best suited for the different types of coffeemakers. The grinds are packaged in vacuum-tight cans or in sealed bags for distribution to the supermarkets or grocery stores. Instant coffee is made from roasted coffee and steamed into a beverage, which is then dehydrated, leaving tiny crystals of strong brewed coffee. When boiling water is added, the crystals dissolve and create the beverage. Freeze-dried coffee is a variation of instant, and since it utilizes a more expensive technology, costs more than regular instant. With freeze-dried coffee, the strong brewed coffee is frozen at extremely low temperatures and then dried in a vacuum to preserve more freshness of the original brew. Decaffeinated coffee is made by steaming the green beans until soft and removing the caffeine from the beans, which are then processed in the conventional manner.

In summary, coffee futures respond to fundamental supply and demand considerations. Most producing countries (Brazil, Colombia, El Salvador, Nicaragua, Panama, Ethiopia, Zaire, and so on) need foreign exchange to pay for oil imports. Consequently, they will continue to export coffee as quickly as they can. This inevitably leads to surpluses and serves as a price depressant. Coffee users are also price sensitive. If coffee approaches $4 per pound, consumption falls off sharply. As a result, the speculator in coffee futures has to exercise great care in devising his or her trading strategy, whether "long," "short," or "spread."

FIGURE 5.

17

The Fundamentals of Sugar

A Summary of Fundamentals

Low Sugar Prices Reflect Record Sugar Production
World sugar production (centrifugal raw value) for the 1981/82 season was forecast at a record 95.8 million metric tons, more than 10 percent above the 1980–81 revised estimate of 86.6 million. Nearly half of the increase comes from improved output in India, Thailand, Turkey, South Africa, Cuba, Poland, and the USSR, all of which had poor crops last year. Although it is estimated that Soviet production will rise by 200,000 tons, it will only be slightly above 1980/81. More than a fifth of the world increase arises from the European Community (EC), which will likely turn out a record 14.7 million tons, up by 1.9 million tons (15 percent) from the 1981 season. The EC's harvested area rose nearly 11 percent. Brazil will probably produce 5 percent more sugar this season— close to its target of 8.6 million tons.

World sugar consumption is expected to rise by 3 to 4 million tons, to around 92 million tons, in response to larger supplies, lower prices, and population growth. With global stocks expected to increase by more than 3 million tons, high interest rates encouraging a lower stocks-to-consumption ratio, and competitive corn syrups absorbing more of the sweeteners market, prices were expected to stay low—10 to 14 cents a pound through the rest of 1982. However, the size of the 1982 sugar crop would also significantly affect prices. As 1982 drew to a close, world sugar supplies exceeded sugar consumption by 3 million tons.

In the absence of a domestic program, at the time of this writing it appears that the world market largely determined United States wholesale and retail prices in 1982. Retail prices averaged 33.5 cents a pound in October, down for the tenth consecutive month, from 56.5 cents in December 1980. It should be remembered that more than 100 countries produce sugar. Raw sugar prices ranged from 65 cents a pound in 1974 to between 7 and 10 cents in 1976–78, then to 42 cents in late 1980, and then finished 1982 at 7 cents a pound.

Near-Record U.S. Beet and Cane Sugar Production Occurred in 1982

United States production of cane and beet sugar (excluding Puerto Rico) exceeded 6.25 million short tons (raw value) in 1982, up 10 percent from a year earlier. This sugarbeet crop—nearly 28 million tons—produced about 4 million tons of sugar, up 11 percent. Sucrose recovery didn't fall significantly because of Michigan's wet weather at harvest, nor did a large percentage of Red River Valley beets frozen in the field, nor did a relatively long processing season at several plants in the Great Plains reduce production. The sugarcane crop—30 million tons—yielded 3 million tons of cane sugar, up 9 percent.

In 1983 United States sugar output could fall 10 to 15 percent, assuming normal yields and reduced acreage, because of low world prices. With a domestic support program, the decline might be only half as much.

Sugar Deliveries Continue Declining

United States sugar deliveries totalled 10 million short tons (raw value) in 1981, down 4 percent from 1980. This implied a per capita consumption of refined sugar of almost 80 pounds, down 4 pounds from 1980. It is important to remember that most of the average American's annual consumption of sugar (80 pounds in 1982) is consumed as a sweetener in commercially prepared food and soft drinks.

Sugar Imports Increased in 1981 and 1982

As recent trends continue, United States sugar imports in 1981 reached 5 million tons (raw value, including shipments from Puerto Rico), up 100,000 tons from 1980. Importers and refiners brought in a large amount of sugar at the end of 1981 in anticipation of a new price support program. Raw sugar imports increased in 1982 by 15 percent, mostly in response to a large drop in United States exports in 1982.

United States Sugar Exports Rose Sharply in 1981, Declined Dramatically in 1982

United States sugar exports reached a record 1 million tons in 1981, up from 650,000 tons in 1980 and only 18,000 tons in 1979. Exports went to Mexico, Peru, Turkey, India, Venezuela, and several other countries. About 96 percent of these exports were in the form of refined sugar. Low world sugar prices, particularly those for the EC's discounted refined sugars, discouraged United States exports in 1982.

Corn Sweetener Use Up—Prices Decline

The United States corn wet-milling grind was 535 million bushels in 1982, up about 7 percent from 1981. Shipments of corn sweeteners for food use totalled around 5.5 million short tons (dry basis), over a third of total caloric sweetener use in 1982. HFCS shipments hit 3 million tons in 1982, up around 12 percent from 1981. Glucose corn syrup shipments showed a slight increase to nearly 2.1 million tons, and dextrose stayed at around 400,000 tons, the same annual level as during 1979–81. Corn sweetener prices declined along with those for sugar in 1981. During 1982, prices averaged close to 1981 levels, with glucose syrup slightly higher.

We should remember that the current price support program is designed to protect the domestic sugar industry from competition abroad. The program provides a floor under which the price of domestically produced sugar cannot fall. The 1981 Farm Bill mandated a sugar loan level of 17 cents a pound.

As this is being written, a controversy is indeed raging. On one side, sugar refiners in this country argue that the government-enacted sugar quotas deny overseas exporters access to United States markets, thereby keeping the price of domestic sugar artificially inflated. Proponents claim the quotas are necessary to ensure the long-term viability of the sugar industry in the United States.

Abundant Cocoa Supplies—Increased Use

Early prospects point to another record world cocoa crop of 1.73 million metric tons, up 4 percent from last year. World grindings are forecast to be well below production, indicating a stock buildup for the fifth straight season. Low cocoa prices have pushed up domestic use and imports this year, and the momentum is expected to carry into 1983.

United States Honey Production Down— Imports Up

United States honey production in 1981 was 180 million pounds, down about 10 percent from 1980. Production in 1982 was 170 million pounds. Imports reached a record 80 million pounds, up from 66 million in 1976. Domestic honey prices averaged slightly under 57.4 cents a pound, the loan rate for the 1981 production. 1982 prices were 55 cents a pound.

As is the case with coffee, most sugar producers are developing countries sorely in need of foreign exchange to pay for oil imports. As a result, sugar availability often exceeds demand. However, the following trading scenario is offered to would-be speculators:

Entry: 11.00 cents per lb.
Exit: 19.00 cents per lb.
Profits Objective: 8 cents per lb. per contract
Risk: 1.5 cents per lb.
Profit-to-loss ratio of 5 to 1
(1 cent per lb. is equivalent to $1,120.00 per contract.)

18

A Perspective on Cotton

General Characteristics

Cotton is the most important textile fiber. Growth in cotton consumption is constrained by competition with manmade fibers, especially polyester. The demand for cotton products is positively stimulated by the growth of population and real income. Cotton is typically grown in combination or rotation with other crops and must compete for land and other inputs on the basis of its relative profitability to producers.

The Market

Size of Cotton Crop

- The U.S. crop year runs from August 1 to July 31.
- The actual U.S. cotton crop for 1980–81 will approximate 11MM bales.
- 5MM will be sold to domestic mills (Milliken, Stevens, Dan River, Burlington, and so on) in North Carolina and South Carolina.

And

- 6MM will be exported to foreign mills, principally in China, Japan, and South Korea.
- The value of the 1980–81 cotton crop will approximate $4 billion, based on an average price of 76 cents per pound.
- The 1981–82 forecast for the U.S. cotton crop is 14MM bales, worth an estimated $5 billion.
- The U.S. cotton crop is harvested starting in July along the Texas panhandle. The growers pick and gin the cotton into 500-lb. bales. The

Memphis merchants have buying offices throughout the cotton belt. The merchants contract for this cotton and have it shipped into bonded warehouses. They borrow from the banks to pay the growers, securing the loans with the warehoused cotton. As the merchants sell the cotton to domestic and international mills, they retire the bank loans.

World Summary

In the face of continued poor economic prospects, the 1981–82 raw cotton consumption by many world textile industries was below expectations. In spite of the current situation, however, consumption during 1981–82 did increase nearly 2 percent, to 66.5 million bales, an indication of underlying strength of demand for cotton or cotton blend textile products, especially in centrally planned economies. It would seem that during the current period of plentiful supplies (the largest world cotton crop on record), and subsequent low prices, textile manufacturers might find themselves in a favorable position. The essential element missing is dependable short-term demand, which translates into some hesitation on the part of raw cotton consumers.

This is true even for some of the strongest textile-producing nations, such as Japan and Korea. Most of the major consumer-importer nations of the Far East showed only modest cotton consumption growth in 1982, and in Western Europe, especially in the European Community (EC), little if any growth was anticipated. Two major adjustments in 1981–82 consumption were noted. India's estimate was reduced by 200,000 bales, and the United States estimate dropped by 100,000 bales. An exception to this guarded approach is China, where prospects for consumption in 1981–82 were still optimistic. However, export competition from the Middle East reversed this optimism at the end of 1982.

World cotton trade reflects consumption prospects. Despite lower prices by major exporters, shipments by December 1982 had not achieved expected levels. The 20.4-million-bale figure in 1981–82 was slightly above the 1980–81 level. However, the outlook did change for a few countries. In the Western Hemisphere, both Colombian and Salvadoran export sales were down from previous estimates. In Africa, an increase in the 1981–82 Egyptian sales level offset a reduction in Senegal.

United States October cotton exports for 1981 exceeded October, 1980 figures, for the first time in the 1981–82 season. October, 1981, exports totaled 274,000 bales, 10 percent above a year earlier, and 21 percent above the 1974–78 average. However, 1982 was dismal at 650,000 bales. Total 1981–82 United States cotton exports reached 7.0 million bales, 1.1 million more than 1980–81. Leading 1981–82 markets for United States cotton were Korea, Japan, China, Canada, and Taiwan. 1982–83 saw United States cotton exports fall dramatically, however, to 6 million bales.

The 1981–82 and 1982–83 estimates for world stocks were increased as larger Soviet production and reduced Indian consumption forecasts translated into larger carryover stocks. Ending stocks for the 1981–82 and 1982–83 seasons came in at 27 million bales. Foreign stocks rose as higher carryin levels for France and Greece boosted European stocks. Historical adjustments in Indonesia and Nigeria also contributed to the larger foreign figure.

The cost, insurance, and freight (CIF) prices in North Europe, as measured by Liverpool Index "A," declined about 6 cents per pound in November, 1981. Faltering economic conditions worldwide are making it difficult for the textile trade to move inventories profitably and, despite favorable cotton prices, demand remains limited. Generally, all cotton growths, including American growths, have declined by a similar amount. As a result, United States cotton remains competitive in the world marketplace.

Prices fell on the New York Cotton Exchange as lack of new fundamental information allowed the bearish mood of the commodity markets to dominate. March futures had fallen to 62.62 cents per pound by December 11, 1981, or more than 100 points, in the first two weeks of December, 1981. This was about the pricing level for all of 1982.

The recurring theme in tropical commodities is that some major producers of cotton will continue to produce at record rates, despite an overabundance of product. This continues to have a long-term depressing effect on cotton prices. However, as opportunities are perceived, the following "long" strategy could be implemented:

ENTRY:	65.00 cents per lb.
EXIT:	80.00 cents per lb.
PROFIT OBJECTIVE:	15 cents per lb. per contract.
RISK:	2 cents per lb. per contract.
PROFIT-TO-LOSS RATIO:	7.5 to 1.

(1 cent per lb. is equivalent to $500.00 per contract)

19

Orange Juice
as a Commodity

The Florida orange industry has been one of the most rapidly expanding and changing commodity systems in U.S. agribusiness. The growth of production of this crop has been phenomenal, from 10 million boxes in the 1920s to more than 170 million boxes in 1976. The cultivation of this crop is concentrated in a few major producing counties in Florida, which produced about three-quarters of the total U.S. crop in 1976.

U.S. Orange Production in 1975–76

	Arizona	California	Florida	Texas	Total
Millions of Boxes	3.9	49.0	172.0	5.8	230.7

The Growing Cycle

Unlike other agricultural products such as wheat and soybeans, Florida orange production has to be planned years in advance.

It takes about four years before a young nursery tree bears its first fruit and eight years until it reaches full maturity.

Groves are productive for sixty to seventy years, but productivity begins to decline after trees reach thirty years of age. Accordingly, tree damage such as that caused by the recent freeze can take several years to correct, even assuming normal conditions thereafter.

Raw oranges mature in Florida over a 9-month period, commencing in September and lasting through May. Early and midseason oranges mature between September and February, while Valencias (late season) are harvested from late February through June. Of the three seasonal varieties of oranges, it is the Valencia that is most significant for concentrate processing. Early and midseason oranges are high in acid content and low in sugar, while the Valencia's proportional content of acid and sugar is the exact opposite. These juices are blended together, under the strict quality standards and supervision of the Florida Citrus Commission, and, after processing, are converted into frozen orange juice concentrate or chilled single-strength orange juice.

The chief hazard in orange production is frost. A severe freeze (temperatures below 26 degrees Fahrenheit for more than four hours) in December, 1962, resulted in a crop of about 75 million boxes when preseason forecasts indicated a 120-million-box potential. The following year, 1963–64, the harvest was further reduced to about 58 million boxes, largely due to tree wood damage caused by the 1962 freeze. However, since wood damage becomes evident in the spring following a freeze, crop forecasts for the 1963–64 season projected an output of 64 million boxes. Thus, as noted, severe freezes can affect several seasons of production, although the carry-over effects can be reasonably well predicted.

The Florida Orange Economy

Supply

The Florida orange industry has encouraged improved production technology through its cooperation with the University of Florida, Florida Citrus Mutual (a grower cooperative), and the Florida Citrus Commission. The development of mechanical harvesting devices, improved fertilizer application, and grove technology have greatly aided growers in raising production.

This is apparent over the last decade. In 1968–69, Florida produced 118 million boxes of oranges for processing, and 108 million gallons of frozen concentrated orange juice (FCOJ). By 1974–75, 165 million boxes of oranges were processed, and produced approximately 178 million gallons of FCOJ. While the total amount of grove acreage under commercial cultivation is believed to have declined somewhat due to urban encroachment, the yield per acre has increased. In 1970–71, grove yield averaged 213 boxes per acre (19,170 lbs.) as compared with 284 boxes per acre (25,560 lbs.) in 1974–75. By the end of 1982, grove yield had grown to 350 boxes per acre.

Consumption

In the past, the rapid expansion of Florida orange production has not resulted in prolonged periods of depressed price levels. Although temporary corrections due to the adverse impact of serious weather (hurricanes, freezes) have helped, it is changes in consumption that have maintained price levels. Primarily responsible for the maintenance of price levels was the technological breakthrough of the development of frozen orange juice concentrate and the increased demand for FCOJ after World War II.

The expansion of orange concentrate production was rapid in the late 1940s and early 1970s, and since then has approximately equalled population growth in the United States. This population growth, however, seems to have slowed considerably, and per capita consumption of FCOJ has begun to level off as well. There is also growing competition from synthetic orange drinks, such as Tang and Awake.

Actually, the per capita level of total orange food consumption has remained relatively unchanged; rather, it is the form of consumption that has changed dramatically, as the following suggests:

U.S. Per Capita Consumption of Oranges

	1946	1961
Frozen Concentrate Form	.2 lbs.	33.4 lbs.
Canned	16.2	5.7
Chilled Juice	—	3.9
Fresh Form	41.5	15.7
	58.3 lbs.	58.7 lbs.

The relationship of processed to unprocessed orange consumption, expressed in terms of the Florida orange crop, is even more dramatic. In 1963, 78 percent of all Florida orange juice was processed and, by 1975, this amount had risen to 96 percent, with 78 percent of total production becoming FCOJ.

Foreign consumption of frozen orange juice concentrate rose dramatically in the early 1960s, but like consumption in the United States, has leveled off in recent years. In 1962, the United States (primarily Florida) exported 3.6 million gallons of frozen orange juice concentrate. By 1972, this number had risen to 11.0 million gallons and has since that time increased approximately 6 percent annually.

The Cooperatives

The development of the Florida processing industry created a need for some type of coordinated production, processing, and marketing operations in order that the consumer could have a consistent quantity and quality of orange concentrate despite the extremely volatile fluctuations in production and price. The Florida orange industry is a very tightly knit group, and it is nearly impossible for any individual grower or processor to operate independently of industry policies. Perhaps the most visible evidence of the degree of coordination and integration within the orange industry is the complex network of cooperatives. There are many types of cooperatives, whose members may include growers, processors, private companies, and other co-ops.

Today, cooperative agreements offer orange growers several advantages, including:

1. The grower who is a co-op member is guaranteed a market for his or her crop.

2. The farmer is guaranteed a minimum price equal to the Florida Canners Association average-price-per-pound solid.

Most cooperatives work on a "price pool" basis. The cooperative keeps a record of the "solid content" of each grower's deliveries. The cooperative does not price each grower's oranges as they are delivered to the cooperative or processor, but rather pools all the sales over a time period that covers the early varieties for one period and the late varieties for another. In this way each member of the cooperative receives the average price of the pool for the pound-solid quantities he or she delivered. It is no longer important to the grower whether or not his or her crop is delivered at a high-priced or low-priced period of the harvest. The pool enables each member to average out the price swings that can take place within a crop year.

The advantages to the processors are:

1. The processor is guaranteed a supply of a certain number of boxes of oranges.

2. The pool contract keeps average procurement costs in line with competitors' procurement costs, since all are related to the Florida Canners Association price.

3. The processor does not have to pay the growers until payment is received for his or her output.

Many arrangements have been devised by processors to improve their coordination within the total Florida orange system. In order to improve procurement operations by maintaining a flow of raw material to the plant, some processors have resorted to backward integration in the form of actual grove ownership, or leasing of orange groves and so on.

Processors have also attempted to reduce the market uncertainties affecting their output by entering into retail volume contracts, whereby, for example, a processor would "can" its output for A & P under the A & P label.

Advantages of the retail volume-shipment contracts to the processors are:

1. The processors are guaranteed a market for a certain volume of their orange concentrate.

2. The processors receive storage payment from the retailer on invoiced merchandise that remains in the processors' warehouses.

3. The processors are guaranteed approximately equal monthly shipments of their products and also guaranteed prompt payment of invoiced concentrate.

The retailer benefits from the arrangement in the following ways:

1. The processors guarantee to deliver specified quantities of frozen orange concentrate.

2. The retailer gets free storage on all concentrate invoiced until January 15 of the season.

3. The retailer is guaranteed a quality USDA-inspected product. More importantly, the retailer's cost is guaranteed to be no more than that of any other retailer on date of invoicing or shipment.

In late 1981 orange juice futures were trading at $1.50 per lb. Naturally, this product moves dramatically in response to cold weather and prospects of cold weather in January as the crop was about to be harvested. Speculators usually take a "long" position in orange juice futures on reports of frost, liquidating those positions as soon as a profit objective is achieved. The fact that Brazil is a major exporter of product to the United States also keeps the price of the futures contract from running away.

VI
THE FEED COMPLEX

20

The Grain Industry

The production, distribution and processing of grain and oilseeds by U.S. firms represents a multibillion dollar industry. Specifically the wheat, corn, and soybean industries will be examined here, with lesser crops such as barley, sorghum grain, oats, flaxseed, rye, and so on not being specifically addressed. It should be noted, however, that many of the major grain companies also trade in these lesser crops.

I. Production Overview

WHEAT: Wheat is divided into five classes: hard winter wheat, soft red winter wheat, hard spring wheat, durum, and white wheat. Total wheat supply for the 1981–82 season was projected at 3.3 billion bushels, of which approximately 25 percent is projected for domestic use and the remainder for export. Assuming an average price of $4.00 per bushel, the value of wheat consumed domestically and exported will be approximately $9.5 billion.

HARD WINTER WHEAT: Represents the largest wheat class and is grown in the Plains states: Colorado, Kansas, Nebraska, Oklahoma, Texas. Kansas is by far the largest grower. The wheat has a high protein content and is primarily used for bread and quality baking flour. This class is deliverable on the Kansas City Board of Trade.

SOFT RED WINTER WHEAT: A lower protein wheat, which is grown in the central and southern states. It is the second largest wheat class in terms of production. Use is primarily in cookie and cake manufacturing. This class is deliverable on the Chicago Board of Trade.

WHITE WHEAT: Similar to soft red winter wheat in protein and usage. Grown in the Northwest and exported primarily out of the Pacific Coast.

HARD SPRING WHEAT: The highest protein wheat produced. Used in quality breads. Produced in the North Central states: Minnesota, North Dakota, South Dakota. This grade is deliverable on the Minneapolis Grain Exchange.

DURUM: Used in producing semolina, which is used in the production of macaroni products. Grown in the same area as the hard spring wheat.

The winter wheats are planted in the fall and harvested in the summer, while the spring wheats are planted in the spring and harvested in late summer. The majority of domestic grain is either exported or milled into flour. It was projected that export in the 1981–82 season would represent 64 percent of total usage, with milling representing another 26 percent. The remainder of the usage is divided between feed and seed. The major export markets are the USSR, China, Japan, Eastern Europe, Brazil, Egypt, Iran, and South Korea. Other major exporting countries are Argentina, Canada, Australia, and the members of the European Economic Community.

CORN: The total corn supply for the 1981–82 season was projected at 8.3 billion bushels, of which 4.9 bushels were to be used domestically, and 2.5 billion exported. Assuming an average price of $3.40 per bushel, the value of corn consumed domestically and exported was to be approximately $16.5 billion. The two major classes of corn are yellow corn and white corn, with yellow being by far the predominant class. The major growing areas are the central states, that is, Iowa, Illinois, Minnesota, and Nebraska. Corn is planted in the spring and is harvested in the fall. Domestically, the primary use of corn is for feed, either directly to livestock or after being processed by milling concerns. Processed corn is also used for food and the production of high-fructose corn syrup. Another potential market for corn is in the production of ethanol for gasahol. Recently this area has been receiving greater attention. The major export markets for corn are Japan, Russia, Spain, West Germany, Italy, Poland, Taiwan, and Korea.

SOYBEANS: The total soybean supply for the 1981–82 season was projected at 2.2 billion bushels, of which 1.2 billion bushels were to be used domestically and 800 thousand bushels exported. Assuming an average price per bushel of $7.90, the value of soybeans consumed domestically and exported in the 1980–81 season was to approximate $15.5 billion. The classes of soybeans are yellow, green, brown, and black, with the predominant class being yellow. The major growing areas for soybeans are the Midwest and South Central states, with the leading producers being Illinois and Iowa. Soybeans are planted in the late spring and harvested in late fall. The soybean has little commercial use in itself, however, when processed soybean meal and oil are derived. Soybean meal is a high-protein livestock feed that is finding increasing use as a protein and mineral fortifier in baking goods and sausage meats. Soybean oil, after being refined, is used in vegetable shortenings, margarines, salad oils, and so on, and also has industrial usage in oil, paints, varnishes, and so on. The major export markets for soybeans are Japan, the Netherlands, West Germany, and Spain. Brazil and Argentina are other major soybean producers.

APPROACH TO INDUSTRY

As stated in the preceding section, the industry was to consume or export crops with a projected market value of more than forty billion dollars in 1982. This, of course, does not include the value added in processing and transportation. A market of this size obviously has immense financing requirements. One method of approaching this market is to follow the crops through the marketing and processing stages and identify the major firms active in each area. Generally speaking, the crops move after harvest to storage and then either into processing or export markets, or they are consumed directly as live-stock feed. Listings were developed of the leading firms in the follow-ing sectors of the industry: a) storage, merchandising, and export; b) flour milling; c) dry corn milling; d) wet corn milling; e) soybean processing.

III. Storage, Merchandising, and Export

Total storage capacity of grain in the United States as of 1980 was approximately 7.1 billion bushels of which 1.6 billion bushels was represented by licensed terminal, subterminal, river, and port elevators. The top end of elevator operators is represented by such integrated firms as Pillsbury, General Mills, Continental Grain, Cargill, Bunge, Peavey Company, Early and Daniels, Archer Daniel Midland, and so on. In addition, firms such as A.E. Staley, Anderson Clayton and Com-pany, and Ralston Purina are also included in this listing. Private, less integrated, firms such as the Anderson, Lincoln Grain; CGF Grain; Garvey Elevators; and Bartlett and Company also represent a large segment of storage capacity. From conversations with firms in the industry, it appears that the firms controlling a majority of the storage are also the predominant merchandisers both domestically and for export. Although no figures are compiled, it is commonly understood that the five major exporters are Cargill, Continental Grain, Bunge, Louis Dreyfus, and Garnac Grain. In addition, firms such as Algred C. Toepfer, the subsidiary of Germany's largest grain firm of the same name; Tradigrain, staffed by former Cook Industry employees; and Gulf Coast Grain, and the United States Grain Corporation, subs of Mitsui, are reported to be active in the export.

The following represents an overview of the services provided by the elevator, merchandiser, and exporter, and identifies certain common industry practices and risks. It must be pointed out that the industry is extremely complex and the following represents a very general broad brush approach.

Elevators

Grain that moves into merchandising channels is normally first purchased from the producer or stored for the producer by a country elevator. The grain is usually brought to the elevator by truck. A sample is weighed and graded, and the grain is either purchased or stored by the elevator. If stored for the producer, a warehouse receipt is issued by the elevator. Normally the weighing, sampling, and inspection at country elevators is not done by individuals employed by official agencies. The grading of the grain is critical, as prices are based on the grade. Such things as test weight per bushel, damaged kernels, foreign material, moisture content, and so on are considered when determining the appropriate grade.

In addition to grade, wheat is also classified by protein level, with the higher proteins usually being traded at premiums. Wheat and corn are graded from number 1 to number 5 plus a United States sample grade that does not meet the grades 1–5 requirements. Grade number 1 is the most favorable. Soybeans are classified by grades 1–4, with a United States sample grade for those that do not meet the grades 1–4 requirements. During the period of time that the grain is stored, it is important for the elevator to maintain the quality of the grain, as it is responsible for delivering to the receipt holder a specific amount and quality of grain. In addition to grain storage, the country elevator provides drying, cleaning, scalping, and automatic sampling for which fees are normally charged. The elevator also uses its drying and cleaning equipment to improve the grade of grain it purchases for its own account, which enables it to receive a better price on resale.

Two major risks that are associated with the storage of grain are quality deterioration and the possibility of the grain being destroyed, that is, through fire and elevator explosion. The maintenance of grain quality and condition is a function of warehouse management and proper equipment, and is probably best evaluated by observing the experience of the warehouse and through checking with other firms in the industry. According to our industry sources, deterioration of the grain through explosion, fire, and so on can be covered by insurance and can also be reduced by proper operating procedures. Research is actively being done on the causes of grain explosions, and equipment is being designed to reduce the levels of grain dust, to better ventilate elevators, and to better measure concentration of gases and vapors. The insurance that is maintained should cover both the value of the real estate and grain, as well as the business interruption.

TERMINAL, SUBTERMINAL, AND RIVER ELEVATORS: The next step in the merchandising chain usually involves the grain moving directly into the processing industries; or being sold as feed; or being sold to terminal, subterminal, or river elevators. These elevators usually have a larger storage capacity and more efficient grain handling equipment than the country elevators and are situated on major transportation lines. These elevators serve the purpose of aggregating grain in convenient locations for bulk movement into export channels or domestic processing. Purchases are usually made from country elevators or merchandisers, and grain is stored for merchandisers and processors. When the grain leaves the country elevator, it is weighed and graded before a bill of lading is issued by the carrier. If the elevator is not an official station, the grain is again weighed and graded en route at an official station. The official weight and grade are then sent along with a draft to the terminal elevators. The drafts are pro forma, calling for a 90 percent payment of the contract price. When the grain is received at the terminal elevator, it is again weighed and graded, and the remainder of the draft is paid. The drafts are normally documentary sight drafts and are collected through banking channels. The use of a negotiable bill of lading allows the grain to be traded frequently while en route. The terminal elevators represent the major inland storage facilities, and certain elevators are designated as good for delivery on the grain exchanges. Grain can be received at these elevators by truck, rail, or barge, and one important factor in their success is the equipment and capacity they have to receive and load-out grain. Normally at these elevators, grain is sampled, weighed, and graded by either employees of official agencies or by employees licensed under the United States Grain Standards Act. When these as well as other requirements are met, the weights and grades are considered official and are used in conducting trade. The terminal elevators provide the same services as country elevators, and the major risks associated with storage are the same.

EXPORT ELEVATORS: The main function of the export elevator is to move the grain from the inland transportation, that is, rail, barge, or truck, and place it on ships. A fee is charged for this service, which is known in the industry as "fobbing." The fee is a per bushel charge, and therefore, the elevator's capacity to unload and load the grain is crucial. To increase utilization, elevators will enter into through-put agreements with shippers, in which the shipper agrees to process a certain amount of grain through the elevator. Storage represents a minor portion of the operations of the export elevator as income to the export vessel. As the grain leaves the elevator and falls into the vessel, it is weighed and graded, based on a sample, and a mates receipt is issued. The mates receipt is the title document. The mates receipt is then exchanged for a bill of lading. Export elevators provide the same services as the terminal and country elevators.

LICENSING OF ELEVATORS: Elevators may be licensed by either the state or federal government, or by both. Federal licensing is authorized under the United States Warehouse Act and is the responsibility of the Department of Agriculture. The following is a summary of the act and the requirements for federal licensing. The information was taken from a paper prepared by the USDA. The act is administered by the Warehouse Division, Agricultural Marketing Service, USDA, headquartered in Washington, DC.

The division spends about half its time in administering the United States Warehouse Act and the other half on programs of the Commodity Credit Corporation. Currently licensed under the act are approximately 250 cotton warehouses, 1,800 grain elevators, and seventy warehouses storing other agricultural commodities. These represent about 60 percent of the commercial cotton storage capacity and about 42 percent of the commercial grain elevator space in this country. At any given time, the aggregate value of warehouse receipts—representing the actual stored products in federally licensed warehouses—may be $8 billion or more.

To qualify for a license, a warehouseperson must have a suitable and properly equipped warehouse; a good business reputation; and a minimum net worth, computed according to warehouse capacity and the type of commodity stored. He or she must furnish an acceptable bond in an amount fixed by the USDA; have qualified personnel with knowledge of how to weigh, inspect, and grade agricultural products; have adequate equipment to properly grade and weigh; apply on a prescribed form signed by an authorized officer; and pay initial inspection and license fees.

To the extent of their capacity, licensed warehouses are required under the act to receive for storage agricultural products of the kind customarily stored, which are tendered in the usual manner in the ordinary and usual course of business and in a suitable condition for warehousing. Warehouses must not discriminate between persons desiring to avail themselves of warehouse facilities.

The act requires licensed warehousepersons to issue receipts for all stored products as evidence to the depositor that his or her products are in storage. All such receipts, printed under government contract, must be ordered from the USDA.

A warehouse receipt may be issued only when the products are actually received in the licensed warehouse. Negotiable receipts must be surrendered to the warehouseperson and cancelled by him or her before the products may be delivered.

Each licensed warehouseperson is required to post a tariff or schedule of charges, setting forth the amount the warehouse charges for receiving, delivering, storage, insurance, conditioning, and all other warehousing services. Copies must be furnished to USDA and are subject to disapproval if exorbitant or discriminatory. Before making any changes in rates, a warehouse must submit amended tariffs to the USDA, and these are also subject to disapproval.

Receipts issued under the United States Warehouse Act are supported by inspection and weight certificates issued by warehouse inspectors and weighers licensed under the act. Licenses are now in effect for more than 10,000 inspectors and weighers, who are usually employees of the licensed warehouseperson, but can be employees of an independent agency. Their "service licenses" enable them to perform duties only at the facilities of the licensed warehouseperson. No direct supervision is made of their daily operations by USDA personnel. The certificates they issue are not valid for purposes of the United States Grain Standards Act (under which grain is inspected and graded) unless they also hold a grain inspector's license under that act.

Applicants for service licenses are required to furnish five character references and a 10-year work resume, and must demonstrate their ability to properly inspect and/or weigh grain.

The United States Warehouse Act is administered mainly through a program of comprehensive warehouse examinations—about twice each year on an unannounced basis. Examiners review the warehouseperson's obligations to depositors, as represented by outstanding warehouse receipts, scale tickets, and accounts. They inventory all the commodities on hand, comparing this to the record of obligations.

They also review a warehouseperson's recordkeeping, housekeeping practices, sanitation, and insurance coverage, and they check the quality of the product in storage. When minor discrepancies or adverse conditions are found, warehousepersons are asked to bring operations into compliance within fifteen days. When violations are considered serious, the warehouseperson's license may be suspended. The act provides penalties of up to ten years in prison and up to a $10,000 fine for improprieties in connection with warehouse receipts or inspection and weighings.

Information has not been compiled on individual state regulations, however discussions with firms in the industry indicate that several states have more stringent regulations than the federal government. Reportedly Kansas has the best-regulated elevators.

GRAIN EXCHANGE ELEVATORS: Each one of the three grain exchanges has designated elevators that are acceptable for delivery of the
particular grain being traded. Before an elevator is declared "regular"
for delivery on the Chicago Board of Trade, it must be inspected by the
CBOT. The exchange may require that all grain in the elevator be
removed and inspected and graded, and that new receipts be issued.
The elevator must also have appropriate rail facilities and must have
adequate equipment for the receiving, handling, and shipping of grain
in bulk. Appropriate bonds and insurance must be in place, and the
warehouse must be in good financial standing. Records must be maintained of all grain received and delivered daily by grade and of grain
remaining in store at the end of the week. The warehouses are inspected at least twice a year by the exchange. The warehouses that are
designated as "regular" for delivery of corn, wheat, and soybeans are
located in switching districts in Chicago (47.3 MM bushels), Toledo
(45.4 MM bushels), and St. Louis (16.9 MM bushels) and are elevators of
the major grain merchandisers and cooperatives. All warehouse receipts
that are eligible for delivery on the CBOT must be registered with the
exchange, and the exchange verifies signatures.

KANSAS CITY BOARD OF TRADE: In order for a warehouse to be
"regular" for delivery on the Kansas City Exchange, it must be licensed
as a public warehouse by the federal government, or Kansas, or
Missouri, and its capacity must be at least 100 bushels. The elevator
must have appropriate facilities and rail connections and be of un-
questioned financial standing. At a minimum, its net worth should be
15 cents per bushel, based on aggregate capacity. The elevator must be
appropriately bonded and insured. The elevator's status as "regular"
for delivery must be renewed annually. Total capacity for deliverable
grain is 84.2 million bushels.

MERCHANDISING: An integral part of elevator operations is the merchandising of grain. The aim of the elevator is to use its capacity to the
fullest extent. This is done by turning over the grain as quickly as
possible and only storing grain when it is necessary from a marketing
viewpoint or in order to use existing capacity. Ideally, the elevator,
when purchasing grain, would like to immediately be able to sell the
grain at a price that would cover its handling charges and provide a
profit. This is not always possible, however, as the elevator must be
able to service its customers and is, therefore, forced to buy when they
are ready to sell. In this event, the elevator has the ability to hedge its
purchase on one of the grain exchanges. Normally, elevators will be
constantly in touch with other elevators and merchandisers, receiving
bids for grain to be delivered at specific locations at specific times. The
elevator can then discount transportation and interest charges and
know what to bid for grain. If there are no active buyers, the elevator

can use the prices quoted on the grain exchanges as the base from which to discount transportation and interest costs. As the price of grain can be extremely volatile, and the elevators and merchandisers trade large amounts of grains in relation to their capital, their merchandising and hedging policies are of critical importance.

Merchandising Risk

There appear to be three aspects to the merchandising risk.

1. Credit
2. Contract Cancellations
3. Position Risks

CREDIT: Generally speaking, supplier credit is not extended in the industry. Domestic sales are normally on sight draft against documents. The drafts are drawn for 90 percent of the contract value and are accompanied by bills of lading, weight certificate, certificate of grade, and other necessary shipping documents. These drafts are normally collected through bank channels; thus the seller does not release the title document (bill of lading) until the draft has been paid. This drafting procedure reduces the credit risk associated with domestic transactions. The credit exposure taken by the seller is reduced to the 10 percent of the invoice price not covered by the draft. This 10 percent is paid by the buyer after weighing and sampling the grain. While in theory this 10 percent should be outstanding for a short period of time, transportation and paperwork delays may, according to industry sources, cause this payment to be deferred for a number of months. Bulk shipments are normally made by rail or barge. A normal hopper carries 3,500 bushels, while a barge will carry 43,000 bushels. Rail shipments of seventy-five cars are now being made, due to transportation discounts, and multibarge shipments may be sold to substantial customers. The significance of this 10 percent exposure is obviously dependent upon the capital of the selling firm and the size of the transaction. International transactions are normally shipped on confirmed or advised letters of credit (sight or time) or cash against documents. If time drafts under letters of credit are used, the drafts are normally discounted without recourse by a bank. Credit exposure is therefore limited to the instance in which the advising bank refuses to negotiate drafts although properly presented under a letter of credit. This exposure represents a sovereign and foreign bank risk that is similar to the risk when shipping CAD (cash-against-documents).

CONTRACT CANCELLATIONS: Grain companies commit themselves far in advance of shipment dates to purchase and sell grain. These commitments are normally either hedged or done on a back-to-back basis. Elevators may contract to purchase grain from producers in advance of the harvest, or contract to purchase grain from the other elevators or merchandisers for deferred delivery. In the event that the supplier of the grain defaults, the firm will either have to buy back its hedge or go into the open market and buy the grain. In a rising market, generally speaking, a loss will be sustained equal to the difference between the price at which the buyer contracted to purchase the grain and the open market price. In the event of a buyer's default, the firm could suffer a loss in a declining market. The magnitude of a loss sustained due to a contract cancellation is a function of the size of the commitment and price volatility. Commitments would vary from firm to firm. Between December 1, 1980, and December 10, 1980, the prices of corn, wheat, and soybeans dropped approximately 15 percent, 23 percent, and 20 percent respectively.

POSITION RISK: Whenever grain is purchased or sold, the firm is exposed to a price risk until the transaction is offset by either a physical purchase or sale, or is hedged on one of the future exchanges. In assessing the risk associated in financing elevators or merchandisers, it is important to understand their hedging policy. Some aspects of their policy that should be addressed are the size of the net position that the firm is willing to maintain, the timing between taking a position and offsetting it with a physical or futures transaction, whether weekend positions are maintained, and how physical trading is conducted after the exchanges close. While hedging reduces the price risk associated with carrying inventory, it does not eliminate it.

Once a transaction is hedged, the risk exists that the spread between the futures price and the price of the physical grain will move against the firm. This risk can be highlighted by the following example:

> *April 2*
> Firm purchases 5,000 bushels of wheat at $4.25/bushel
> Firm sells 1 Futures Contract on the CBOT for May delivery for $4.35
>
> *April 10*
> Firm sells 5,000 bushels of wheat at $4.35/bushel−$.10 profit
> Firm buys back May Future at $4.46   −$.11 loss
> Net $.01 loss

If the pricing of the physical grain would have increased more than the price of the May future, a profit would have been made on the hedge. The potential for disparity between price movements of the physical grain and the futures price is especially evident in the case of wheat, which has the three different classes traded primarily on three different exchanges. While soft winter wheat is primarily traded in Chicago, hard winter wheat in Kansas City, and hard spring wheat in Minneapolis, large transactions in all three classes are hedged in Chicago due to that exchange's larger volume. The prices of the three classes at times move independently, which increases the risk of hedging the hard wheats on CBOT. Prices demonstrate variation in the price movement. In connection with a firm's hedging philosophy, its policy toward hedges that are moving against it should also be discussed. One other area that should be mentioned in conjunction with a position risk is basis pricing. Grain firms often enter into contracts to buy or sell at a specific spread over a specific contract month on one of the exchanges, for example, purchase of 40 cents over the May Chicago wheat, soft red wheat at Guld. The hedge is placed by either buying or selling the May Chicago Wheat contract. In the preceding examples a hedge would be placed by selling the May contract. The firm would, therefore, be protected against price movements in the volatile futures market between the time the purchase commitment was made and the physical grain was sold. The price risk is reduced to a basis risk, which is less volatile. Thus, if at the time the grain was sold, the basis dropped to 38 cents over the May future, a 2-cent loss would be incurred.

TRANSPORTATION: The ability to transport grain by the cheapest and most efficient manner is critical to a firm's profitability. The responsibility for providing transportation is dependent upon the terms of sales. The predominant modes of domestic transportation are barge and rail. Hopper cars are the most frequently used to obtain transportation when needed. If the terms of sale require that the grain be in a rail car at the Guld at a specific time, and due to a car shortage a timely delivery is not made, a default may exist. In order to reduce the risk of car shortages and also reduce rail charges, the large firms will lease or buy hopper cars.

The same situation exists with barge transportation, and the larger firms also maintain a fleet of barges. In addition to shortages of transportation, a risk that may be lessened by controlling rail cars and barges, delays in the transportation system represent a separate risk. Barge transportation may be delayed due to low water levels or congestion on the rivers. Rail delays occur primarily when export elevators are unable to process the rail cars quickly enough. The cars get backed up and a rail embargo may be declared. The inland transportation must also be coordinated with the arrival of the export vessel, as demurrage will be incurred if the grain is not in place when the vessel is in port and will also be incurred if the grain arrives early and the rail cars or barge cannot be unloaded. Demurrage charges on large shipments can run up to $8M to $10M per day. In addition, the firm's capacity to load large quantities of grain at a given time will improve margins as freight rates will be reduced. As an example, railroads have recently introduced discounted rates for movement of grain in units of seventy-five cars. A firm that is able to take advantage of this discount can be more competitive than a smaller firm. The major grain firms have departments whose sole responsibility is coordinating transportation.

SUMMARY OF RISKS: In summary, it appears that the major risks associated with elevator and merchandising operations are elevator explosion and fires, which are reduced by proper insurance coverage; grain deterioration, which can be controlled by adequate operating procedures; and inventory losses due to price fluctuations, which can be mitigated by a well-conceived hedging program. Contract defaults also represent a potential risk to a firm, however, defaults are reportedly rare in the industry. The risk associated with receivables, which is common in any industry, is generally reduced to 10 percent of the invoice volume for domestic sales due to their drafting procedure, and normally consists of a country and foreign bank exposure on foreign sales when unconfirmed letters of credit and CAD terms are used. While the industry has developed methods of controlling their exposure to inventory price fluctuations and credit risks associated with their sales, such external factors as weather and transportation are out of its control. Firms within the industry are therefore subject to reduced volume and lower margins due to a poor harvest or transportation delays. As the industry is very competitive, it is important that the grain delivery system be run in an efficient manner or a firm may have the normally thin margins eliminated through excessive demurrage charges, grain deterioration during transportation, and so on.

As with any industry, the risk involved in the industry must be applied to individual firms, thus contract defaults or even the 10 percent credit exposure on receivables may be significant, depending on the size of the firm in relation to the contracts in which it deals.

The potential exists for sudden and severe losses in the merchandising of grain if proper trading policies are not maintained. The demise of Cook Grain, which was one of the largest United States exporters in the mid-70s, and the recently publicized losses of Farmers Export Corporation testify to this fact. It is therefore important, when soliciting firms in this market, to identify their policies with regard to the risks previously mentioned and to determine their reputation in the industry. Obviously the necessary depth of analysis of the firm's trading policies should be determined by its financial strength and activities.

V. Processors
(Grain Converters or Millers)

The processing of grain is becoming concentrated to a greater degree with the large agribusiness firms. Discussions with firms in the industry indicate that the future of the industry lies with the larger firms and that the single processing firm is a dying breed.

FLOUR MILLING: The concentration within the flour milling industry is indicated by the fact that the ten largest flour milling companies account for 70 percent of the industry's wheat flour capacity. In 1975 it was 76 percent. The bulk of the capacity is controlled by the major integrated firms. It should be noted that Centennial Mills, which was a division of Univar Corporation, was recently purchased by Archer, Daniel, Midland. This purchase placed ADM as the country's leading flour miller. Peavey Company also recently announced the construction of a 5,000-daily-CWT mill in Arizona. This additional capacity makes the company the third largest United States miller. In order to get an idea about the difference in size between the seventeen largest private firms and the smaller firms, Seaboard Allied Million, as of May, 1980, had revenues of $406 million, earnings of $5.8 million, and a net worth of $53 million. Cereal Food Processors had revenues for the ten months ending February, 1981, of $64 million, earnings of $78 thousand, and a net worth of $3.6 million. AD&B on Bay State Milling indicated, as of June, 1979, sales of $100 million and capital of $9 million. Seaboard Allied is financed on an unsecured basis and uses the major New York and Chicago banks.

INDUSTRY OVERVIEW: It is anticipated that 605 million bushels of wheat will be used for food in 1981, the majority of which will be milled for flour. This represents approximately $2.4 billion of wheat that will be processed. Mills are normally established to process particular classes of wheat, which flour is used for different purposes. Hard winter and spring wheat produces a flour suitable for quality breads due to its high protein content. Soft winter wheat is used to produce flour for baking and cookie and cracker manufacturers, while durum wheat produces semolina, which is used in the manufacture of pasta products. The extraction rate from the wheat is approximately 72 percent, with the remaining 28 percent classified as millfeed, which is used in animal feed. The millers will purchase grain directly from farmers, elevators, or merchandisers, and normally have elevator capacity at the mill to store the grain prior to processing. The grain is normally purchased on sight draft terms from the elevators and merchandisers. The flour is then sold to bakers or jobbers, on draft or open-account terms of up to sixty days, or, for the larger firms, retailed under their own name.

Milling firms used to book business out to 120 days, which did not include carrying charges to the buyer. In the recent environment of high interest rates, the free carrying charge period has been reduced to sixty days. The wheat futures markets are actively used by the firms to hedge inventory and purchase and sales commitments. While there is not a futures market for flour, there is an active physical market with prices quoted for the various types of flour. The price of flour is affected by the price of wheat as well as the price of millfeed, which is also traded in physical markets. If the millfeed market is particularly strong, the miller may be able to reduce the price of flour in relation to the income being earned by millfeed sales. One other major factor in a mill's operation is transportation costs. The mill is affected by the cost of transporting grain to its facilities and also the cost of shipping the flour and millfeeds to its buyers. If the firm is able to take advantage of freight discounts through bulk loading, it will better be able to maintain its margin.

CORN MILLING: Two processing methods are used for corn: dry milling and wet milling. The dry milling process produces grits, cereal products, feed, meal, oil, and industrial products. The wet milling process produces, in addition to the products just mentioned, high fructose corn syrup, which is used as a substitute for sugar. Corn will normally produce about 66 percent starch, which is used in making the syrup, 30 percent feed materials, and 3 percent oils. Corn processing is dominated by major firms. Bunge Corporation and Martha White Foods, Inc., which is a division of Beatrice Foods, Inc., are the dominant dry corn mills, with Bunge claiming to be the largest dry miller in the country. CPC, American Maize Products, and A.E. Staley are the primary wet millers. The feed products and high fructose corn syrup, while not traded on a futures exchange, are traded actively in physical markets.

SOYBEAN PROCESSING: The processing of soybeans results in soybean meal and soybean oil, both of which are traded on the Chicago Board of Trade. Trade standards are maintained for soybean meal according to the trading rules of the National Soybeans Processors Association (NSPA). The meal is used primarily as a livestock and poultry feed and is both consumed domestically and exported. The soybean oil that is initially extracted from the soybean must be degummed and refined before it is used for edible or industrial purposes. Grade and quality standards are established by the NSPA for crude soybean oil, and crude degummed soybean oil. The refined oil is primarily used in food processing, although there are industrial uses in the production of soap, varnish, paint, and so on.

It is estimated that out of a sixty-pound bushel of soybeans, the processor gets between ten and eleven pounds of oil, and between forty-seven and forty-eight pounds of meal. The soybean processing industry reflects the type of concentration noted in other milling industries. Between 1951 and 1971, total milling capacity increased from 310 million bushels to 900 million bushels, while the number of plants decreased from 193 to 123. From 1972 through 1979, the capacity increased to 1,350 million bushels, and the number of plants decreased to ninety-four. Of the ninety-four plants, sixty-seven are owned by twelve companies. Although individual plant capacity is not given, the leading processors appear to be Cargill, Central Soya, Archer Daniel Midland, and Ralston Purina. The major soy oil refiners appear to be Anderson Clayton Foods; Hunt Wesson Foods; Best Foods Division of CPC International; PVO International, subsidiary of Kay Corporation; Central Soya; Bunge; ADM; and Cargill.

The basic profitability of a soybean processing operation is reflected in the price relationship between the bean and the meal and oil. This relationship is known as the crushing margin. A wide crushing margin will result in a high utilization of crushing capacity, while a small margin will cause cutbacks in production. The prices of the bean, oil, and meal are determined by world markets, and it is therefore difficult for a company to control its margins. From 1972 to 1981, capacity utilization has averaged 85 percent. Due to the current unfavorable crushing capacity, present capacity utilization is approximately 72 percent. Due to the potential for sharp price swings in the bean, oil, and meal markets, firms normally hedge on the Chicago Board of Trade.

RISKS: Some of the risks associated with the processors are similar to those identified with elevator operators. As both the price of the raw material (corn, wheat, and soybeans) and the end product can fluctuate widely, open positions represent a risk. It is, therefore, useful to understand the company's hedging policy with regard to its inventory and forward commitments. Loss through fire and explosion and deterioration of the grain or end product are risks that can be reduced by proper operating procedures and insurance coverage. Selling terms extended by the processor are generally more liberal than those extended by the grain merchandiser, as open account terms of up to sixty days may be granted to the baker, feed manufacturer, and so on, while the processor will purchase on sight draft terms. Transportation costs are also important, and normally, the greater its control over its transportation, the better the firm is able to maintain its margins.

In the fall of 1982, record crops were recorded in all the grains. Government warehouses were bulging to capacity. Farmers elected not to sell their grain but rather to store it in the hope that prices would recover. Soviet sales were expected to help a bit. However, bankruptcies in the farm belt reached levels not experienced since the Great Depression of the 1930's.

VII
SOME FINAL CONSIDERATIONS

21

Commodity Funds

Public commodity funds evolved from the idea of mutual funds. That is to say that investors would entrust their capital to professional managers who, in return for a fee and a percentage of the profits, would make investments with the purpose of increasing the capital at their disposal. The more common form is organized as a limited partnership. The speculator invests around $5,000 in "units" of the partnership, which are redeemable at net asset value by the partnership. Unlike a position in futures contracts, the speculator can only lose his or her $5,000 investment.

Some risk factors are as follows:

1. Commodity futures trading is speculative. Commodity futures prices are highly volatile. Price movements of commodity futures contracts are influenced by changing supply and demand relationships; weather; government, agricultural, trade, fiscal, and monetary and exchange control programs and policies; national and international political and economic events; and changes in interest rates. In addition, governments from time to time do intervene, directly and by regulation, in certain markets, particularly in currencies and gold. Such intervention is often intended to directly influence prices.

2. Commodity futures trading may be illiquid. Most United States commodity exchanges limit the fluctuations in commodity futures contract prices during a single day by regulations referred to as the "daily price fluctuation limit" or "daily limit." During a single trading day no trades may be executed at prices beyond the daily limit. Once the price of a futures contract has reached the daily limit for that day, positions in that contract can be neither taken nor liquidated. Commodity futures

prices have occasionally moved the daily limit for several consecutive days with little or no trading. Similar occurrences could prevent the partnership from promptly liquidating unfavorable positions and could subject the partnership to substantial losses that could exceed the margin initially committed to such trades. In addition, even if commodity futures prices have not moved the daily limit, the partnership may not be able to execute future trades at favorable prices if little trading in such contracts is taking place. Any governmental imposition of price controls may also inhibit price movements in the commodity markets, to the significant detriment of the partnership.

3. Commodity futures trading is highly leveraged. The low-margin deposits normally required in commodity futures trading permit an extremely high degree of leverage. Accordingly, a relatively small price movement in a commodity futures contract may result in immediate and substantial loss to the investor. For example, if at the time of purchase, 10 percent of the price of the futures contract is deposited as margin, a 10 percent decrease in the price of the futures contract would, if the contract were then closed out, result in a total loss of the margin deposit before any deduction for the trading commission. Thus, like other leveraged investments, any futures trade may result in losses in excess of the amount invested. Although the partnership may lose more than its initial margin in a trade, the partnership, and not the limited partners personally, will be subject to margin calls. The partnership is also subject to the risk of failure of any of the exchanges in which it trades.

4. Commodity futures trading is subject to speculative position limits. The CFTC (the Commodities Futures Trading Commission) and certain exchanges have established limits referred to as "speculative position limits" or "position limits" on the maximum net-long or net-short futures position that any person may hold or control in particular commodities. The CFTC has jurisdiction to establish position limits with respect to all commodities traded in exchanges located in the United States, and any exchange may then impose additional limits on positions on that exchange. These modifications of trades of the partnerships, if required, could adversely affect the operations and profitability of the partnerships.

Most of these partnerships concentrate in currencies, metals, and financial instruments. If the preceding analysis of risks has not deterred you, what follows is a list of the major public commodity funds:

    Chancellor Futures Fund
    Chancellor Financial Futures Fund
    Chancellor Futures Fund II
    LaSalle Street Futures Fund
    Galileo Futures Fund

Dean Witter Reynolds Commodity Partners
Financial Futures Fund
Aries Commodity Fund
Saturn Commodity Fund
Harvest Futures Fund I
Harvest Futures Fund II
Illinois Commodity Fund
Recovery Fund I
Recovery Fund II
The Futures Fund
The Resource Fund
Horizon Futures Fund
Global Futures Fund
Hutton Commodity Partners
E.F. Hutton Commodity Limited Partnership
Lake Forest Futures Fund
Midwest Commodity Fund I
Princeton Future Fund I
Peavey Commodity Futures Fund I
Peavey Commodity Futures Fund II
Commodity Trend Timing Fund
Commodity Venture Fund
Vista Futures Fund
Matterhorn Commodity Partners
Boston Futures Fund I
Boston Futures Fund II
Thomson McKinnon Futures Fund
Thomson Commodity Partners I
Sceptre Futures Fund

22

Sources of Market Information

A good speculator needs to have timely market information at his or her disposal at all times. Here is a list of reports available:

GRAINS—CORN, WHEAT, OATS, AND THE SOYBEAN COMPLEX OF SOYBEANS, SOYBEAN MEAL, AND SOYBEAN OIL.   USDA issues monthly crop production reports through its Crop Reporting Board (CRB). These reports give various field crop information, including prospective plantings, planted acreage yields, and production.

CRB publishes a free report calendar and list. Write for the Crop Report Board Catalog, USDA, Room 0005, Washington, D.C. 20250.

Expected Plantings
Sometime in the spring, USDA releases its *Field Crops—Production, Disposition and Value* report. This report covers all of the major grains. A prospective plantings report is also released then. The report contains expected plantings as of the first of the month for corn, oats, and other spring wheat.

In December, the small grains report indicates acreage, yield, and production of wheat and oats, plus revised data for the previous year.

Quarterly grain stocks reports generally include stocks of all wheat, corn, oats, and soybeans by state. These are released in January, April, June, and October. Because the October release excludes bean stocks, a separate soybean stocks report is issued in September.

USDA publishes a weekly grain market news report containing data about grains inspected for export, barge loading, and prices.

Grain Utilization

Five times yearly, the feed situation reports give statistics about grain utilization and government price support program activities.

For wheat traders, a wheat situation report is published four times yearly. It summarizes wheat fundamentals and gives information about world developments, current outlook, government programs, and prospects for the coming year.

The fats and oils situation reports, issued five times each year, offer professional comment on general economic conditions affecting soybeans and soybean oil. These reports also show yield, disappearance, crushings, and exports.

Monthly agricultural prices reports show prices received by farmers for principal crops. Special articles may also appear.

The annual agricultural prices report in June provides a summary of indexes of prices farmers received and paid the previous year. A crop value report in January offers season average prices and value of production for principal crops.

For $13 a year, USDA offers a *Weekly Weather & Crop Bulletin* summarizing weather and its effect on crops for the previous week. An agricultural statistics report, for $5.60, contains comprehensive current and historical agricultural data.

For almost all commodities, traders might find helpful the monthly *Commitment of Traders in Commodity Futures* report from the Commodity Futures Trading Commission (CFTC). This report gives the open interest of holders of long and short positions in a detailed breakout, according to position type and size.

The Chicago Board of Trade, 141 W. Jackson Blvd., Chicago, Ill. 60604, also is a valuable information source for grains. Besides various brochures for each contract, the exchange publishes a statistical annual for $15.50, listing historical spot and futures prices plus a plethora of other useful data. Contact the Chicago Board of Trade's literature services. It also offers a free weekly statistical summary through its market information department.

MEATS—LIVE CATTLE, FEEDER CATTLE, LIVE HOGS, FROZEN PORK BELLIES, AND ICED BROILER CHICKENS.   In January and July, USDA releases its cattle inventory numbers. These two reports include the number and value of all cattle and calves as of the first of the month by states. Monthly cattle on feed reports reveal the total number of cattle on feed, placements, marketings, and other disappearance for seven selected states. Special 23-state cattle on feed reports issued four times yearly give for twenty-three states the information just mentioned and add expected marketings.

The USDA releases four hogs and pigs reports each year. The March, June, September, and December reports show inventory figures and hog numbers by classes. Also included are expected farrowings and pig crop data for selected periods. The December report adds the number of hog operations by state, and inventory by size groups, for major producing states.

Monthly livestock slaughter reports give the number of head and live weights of cattle, calves, hogs, sheep, and lambs slaughtered, plus red meat production by species and hard production for the nation.

In March, the annual summary details total livestock slaughter and red meat and lard production for the previous year by states.

In April, USDA publishes its *Meat Animals—Production, Disposition and Income* for the previous year. For poultry, a weekly broiler hatchery report shows the number of broiler chicks placed and broiler-type eggs set for the previous week in twenty-one states.

A monthly eggs, chickens, and turkeys report designates the number of layers on hand, the number of eggs per 100 layers, and other data. Special monthly reports offer additional information, such as the number and value of chickens on hand.

Monthly poultry slaughter reports reveal the number of head and pounds slaughtered under federal inspection.

In April, USDA reports on *Poultry—Production, Disposition and Income* for the preceding year. And, annual reports on hatchery production and layers and egg production are offered in March and January, respectively.

For all meats, monthly cold storage reports give figures for holdings of meats and poultry products for the end of the previous month. Regional cold storage holdings reports come out in March.

USDA's Agricultural Marketing Service (AMS) compiles a *Livestock Market News* every week and a *Poultry Market News* three times a week. Each report contains cash market information, such as slaughter estimates, prices, and supply-demand narratives.

For hogs and pork bellies, the hog-corn ratio is available from many nongovernmental sources. USDA's *Weekly Sliced Bacon Production* report indicates pork belly consumption.

The cash live and dressed prices for cattle, hogs, and poultry are available daily in most newspapers and on the agricultural wire services.

The Chicago Mercantile Exchange, 444 W. Jackson Blvd., Chicago, Ill. 60606, lists the meat complex contracts. It offers daily information bulletins for $75 a year. These relate both the futures and cash prices plus other information such as USDA slaughter figures and cold storage movement. A statistical yearbook for $6.50 shows past futures and cash prices. Contact the Chicago Mercantile Exchange's office services division for both publications.

Also relevant to the cattle trade are USDA's pasture and range conditions reports, released nine times a year as part of the crop production reports.

FOODS—SUGAR, COFFEE, COCOA, ORANGE JUICE, AND POTATOES. Weather and international factors such as political tensions, currency stability, income level, and trade policies are especially influential for sugar, cocoa, coffee, and orange juice. Obtaining accurate estimates of foreign coffee, cocoa, and orange juice production is particularly difficult.

USDA releases periodic crop production and crop value estimates for all the food commodities.

A monthly sugar market statistics report lists sugar distribution, prices, stocks, and supply. A weekly sugar distribution report is also available from USDA.

For sugar and coffee, a branch of USDA publishes foreign agricultural circulars that relay statistics and general comments about world production and stocks.

The Census Bureau, Washington, D.C. 20233, issues a report on coffee, called *Green Coffee: Inventories, Imports and Roastings.* For more detailed information, traders might contact the Brazilian Coffee Institute, 767 Fifth Ave., 33rd Fl., New York, NY 10015, and request its free yearbook, called the *Coffee Market in the United States and Canada.*

Reports on weekly main-crop purchases by the market boards of Ghana, West Africa, and Nigeria start in October and reflect the major supply of cocoa available for export.

In October, USDA gives a series of world cocoa production estimates. The Census Bureau also offers a monthly report on United States confectionery stores, which covers the poundage and dollar sales of chocolate items.

List Commodities

The Coffee, Sugar & Cocoa Exchange, 4 World Trade Center, New York, NY 10048, which lists these commodities for trading, releases weekly reviews of prices and the latest domestic statistics about the commodities.

Weekly USDA Crop Production estimates for orange juice begin in October. Weekly movement figures indicate consumption and orange juice imports. A crops values report comes out in January, and a citrus fruits report is offered by USDA in September.

Monthly cold storage reports from USDA indicate frozen orange juice stocks. The Florida Department of Citrus makes its own periodic estimates of Florida's and Brazil's crops.

The New York Cotton Exchange, 4 World Trade Center, New York, NY 10048, lists frozen concentrated orange juice, publishes a daily market and weekly trade report, and issues its weekly commitments of traders' figures.

USDA's July, September, October, and January crop production reports include information about potatoes. A potatoes and sweetpotatoes report in September offers comprehensive data about potato acreage, disposition, and also utilization, value, production, prices, and monthly marketings.

COTTON, FOREST PRODUCTS.   The New York Cotton Exchange reports futures and spot prices plus weekly trade information.

USDA's AMS (Agricultural Marketing Service) issues weekly cotton market news, while the CRB offers prospective plantings reports in the spring and acreage figures in early summer. Crop production reports come out about eight times a year. A crop value report is offered in January.

The Census Bureau releases specific reports about the use of cotton in products and the amount of cotton ginned. Three reports offered include the monthly *Cotton Manmade Fiber Staple & Linters* (consumption stocks and spindle activity), *General Imports of Cotton Manufacturers,* and *Woven Fabrics: Production & Unfilled Orders.*

Housing Rates

For lumber and plywood, the Commerce Department, Fourteenth Street between Constitution Ave. and East Street, NW, Washington, D.C. 20203, offers monthly construction reports with the seasonally adjusted rate of housing starts. Reports from the Census Bureau include *Construction and Housing, Housing Starts,* and *Pulp, Paper and Board.*

Stumpage costs, an indicator of available lumber supplies, represent costs of buying standing timber from government land or maintaining co-owned forests. These figures and others are offered by the Western Wood Products Association, 1500 Yeon Bldg., Portland, Ore. 97204. Other information includes figures on production, orders, shipments, weekly inventories, inland mill sales, and past price summaries. For a free list of publications, request the *Subscription Rates for Statistical Reports,* from the association's statistical department.

USDA's Forest Service gives information about general trends in timber supply and demand. And, the Federal Reserve reports on general economic conditions important to construction.

23

Taxes

COMMODITY TRANSACTIONS

In response to the growing concern that taxpayers were avoiding large amounts of tax by deferring income and changing the character of income by the use of commodity straddles, the Economic Recovery Tax Act of 1981 contains provisions intended to limit the ability of taxpayers to use commodity straddle transactions for these purposes. Because of this Congressional concern with loss transactions, the act does not provide comprehensive rules for taxing the gain side of commodity transactions. Completely different rules apply to various transactions. The new provisions of the act apply to property acquired or positions established after June 23, 1981, for taxable years ending after that date.

Regulated Futures Contracts

Regulated futures contracts (RFC) are contracts executed on regulated United States exchanges. Other exchanges can be designated by the U.S. Treasury. RFC held by the taxpayer at the close of the year are subject to the mark to market rule (that is, treated as sold on the last day of that year), and any gain or loss must be taken into account for the taxable year. The resulting gain or loss is then subdivided; 40 percent is treated as short-term capital gain or loss (maximum 1982 rate of 20 percent), and 60 percent is treated as long-term capital gain or loss (maximum 1982 rate of 12 percent). The effective maximum tax rate is therefore 32 percent.

These rules apply to all RFC transactions, whether or not in straddle form. Gains and losses realized during the year on terminating RFC transactions are also taxed under these rules.

PLANNING POINT: Since the effective date for the RFC rules applies to transactions entered into after June 23, 1981, there are two important elections taxpayers can make for 1982 and all years thereafter.

1. Taxpayers who had RFC on June 23, 1981, could elect to treat them under the new rules. Since the election of the tax treatment could be made after the transaction was closed, taxpayers had a chance to "look back" before making their choice. The time and method of making the election was to be determined by the IRS.

2. Taxpayers who had RFC at any time during 1981 could elect to have the new rules apply for transactions in any year starting before June 23, 1981, and ending after June 22, 1981. Since this election was to be made no later than the date for filing the tax return for the year in question, taxpayers were given an opportunity to "look back" on the second year before making the election for the transaction in the first year. The additional tax from this election could be paid over five years. This election was expected to be advantageous for taxpayers who realized short-term capital gain in RFC transactions prior to June 23, 1981.

Straddles

The Economic Recovery Tax Act of 1981 defines a straddle as offsetting holding positions (other than RFC) with respect to traded personal property other than stock. An offsetting position exists if there is a substantial diminution of the taxpayer's risk of loss from holding any position by reason of holding one or more other positions with respect to personal property. Positions are presumed to be offsetting if:

- They are in the same personal property
- They are in the same personal property, even if in different forms
- They are in debt instruments of similar maturity
- They are in positions sold or marketed as offsetting positions
- The aggregate margin requirement for each position is lower than the sum of the margin requirements would be for each position if they were held separately.

Stock options traded on domestic exchanges with a maximum exercise period of one year are excluded. The act also contains related party rules to prevent tax avoidance, including rules dealing with partnerships.

Straddle losses are taxed as follows:

A. Loss deferral rule: A loss realized on one side of a straddle can only be deducted in excess of the unrealized gain on the other side of the straddle. The deferred loss is carried forward to the succeeding year in which the other side of the straddle is closed out.

B. Wash sale rule: The present wash sale rule disallows losses on transactions in which a substantially identical security is reacquired shortly after the disposition, at a loss, of the initially held security. The act extends the wash sale rule to straddle transactions. For instance, if a taxpayer closes out the loss leg of a straddle and immediately replaces it to remain in a balanced position, the wash sale rule will take precedence over the loss deferral rule, to disallow the deductibility of the loss.

C. Short sale rule: The short sale rule is extended to straddle transactions to prevent the conversion of a short-term gain to a long-term gain. COMMENT: A non-RFC futures contract executed on an ex-
   COMMENT: A non-RFC futures contract executed on an exchange, such as a foreign exchange, can qualify for the new 20 percent capital gain rate after only six months and a day. These non-RFC gains are taxed more favorably than RFC gains.

Mixed Straddles

A mixed straddle is a straddle in which only one side of the position is a RFC and each position forming the straddle is identified as being part of the straddle. For these straddles, the taxpayer may elect to treat the RFC side of the straddle under the loss deferral rule or the wash sale rule. If the taxpayer fails to identify the positions constituting a mixed straddle or does not make the election, the mark to market rules will apply to the RFC side, and the loss deferral and wash sale rules will apply to both sides.

PLANNING POINT: Foregoing the mixed straddle election seems to allow the sophisticated investor some planning opportunities. For example, if the gain side of a straddle transaction is written in the United States, the absence of the election brings the mark to market rules into play. Therefore, the gain is realized for tax purposes at the end of the taxable year and taxed at a maximum rate.

CONSULTING SERVICES

For further information on a program of personal financial development, you may contact me at:

527 East 72nd Street
New York, NY 10021

Glossary

Accumulate: When traders buy a commodity heavily and "take it out of the market."

Actuals: Commodities on hand, ready for shipment, storage, or manufacture.

Afloats: Commodities loaded on vessels and on way to destination. May refer to loaded boats in harbor and about to sail but not to cargoes already at destination.

Arbitrage: Simultaneous purchase and sale of the same quantity of the same commodity in two different markets, either in the same country or in different countries. Used to take advantage of what is believed to be a temporary disparity in prices.

At the market: An order to buy or sell at the best price obtainable at the time the order reached the trading pit or ring.

Basis: The price difference over or under a designated future at which a commodity of a certain description is sold or quoted.

Basis Grade: Specified grade, or grades, named in the exchange's futures contract. Other grades are tenderable subject to price differentials from the basis, or "contract" grade.

Bid: A bid subject to immediate acceptance, made on the floor of an exchange to buy a definite quantity of a commodity future at a specified price. (Opposite of "Offer.").

Break: A quick, extensive decline in prices.

Bulge: A rapid advance in prices.

Buy on Close: To buy at the end of the trading session at a price within the closing range.

Buy on Opening: To buy at the beginning of a trading session at a price within the opening range.

C & F (cost and freight): Cost and freight paid to port of destination.

Carrying Charge: Usually refers to warehouse charges, insurance, and other incidentals, often including interest charge and estimated loss (or gain) in weight. When used in connection with delivery against futures, will include weighing, sampling, taring, checking of weights, repairing, repiling, labor to scales, and so on.

Cash Commodity: The actual physical product, as distinguished from the "future." (See "Spot Commodity.")

CCC: Commodity Credit Corporation.

Certified Stocks, or Certified Supplies: Supplies that have been approved as deliverable grades and often graded as to quality. Such gradings hold good for a specified period or for an indefinite time. Some exchanges list established deterioration schedules.

CFTC: Commodity Futures Trading Commission.

CIF: Cost, insurance, and freight paid or included to port of destination.

Clearances: Total marine shipments of a specified commodity as of a given date from domestic and foreign ports.

Close, The: The period at the end of the trading session officially designated by the exchange during which all transactions are considered made "at the close."

Closing Price (or Range): The price (or price range) recorded during the period designated by the exchange as the official close.

Commission House: A concern that buys and sells actual commodities or futures contracts for the accounts of customers.

Contract Grades: Those grades of a commodity that have been officially approved by an exchange as deliverable in settlement of a futures contract.

Cover: The cancellation of a short position in any future by the purchase of an equal quantity of the same future. (See "Liquidation.")

Crop Year: Period from the harvest of a crop to the corresponding period in following year, as used statistically. U.S. wheat crop year begins June 1 and ends May 31; cotton, August 1–July 31; varying dates for other commodities.

Day Orders: Orders at a limited price are understood to be good for the day only unless expressly designated as an open order or good till cancelled order.

Deliverable Grades: See "Contract Grades."

Delivery: The tender and receipt of the actual commodity, or warehouse receipts covering such commodity, in settlement of a futures contract.

Delivery Month: A specified month within which delivery may be made under the terms of a futures contract.

Delivery Notice: A notice of a clearing member's intention to deliver a stated quantity of a commodity in settlement of a futures contract.

Delivery Points: Those points designated by futures exchanges at which the physical commodity covered by a futures contract may be delivered in fulfillment of such contract.

Differentials: The premiums paid for the grades better than the basis grade and the discounts allowed for the grades lower than the basis grades. These differentials are fixed by the contract terms on most exchanges, but in cotton, commercial differentials of differences apply.

Evening Up: When for any reason traders are completing their transactions by selling in the case of longs or by purchasing in the case of shorts, they are said to be "evening up."

Ex-store: Selling term for commodities in warehouse.

FAQ: Fair average quality.

Farm Prices: The prices received by farmers for their products, as published by the U.S. Department of Agriculture, as of the fifteenth of each month.

First Notice Day: First day on which transferable notices can be issued for delivery in specified delivery month.

FOB: Free on board. Usually covers cost of putting commodities on board whatever shipment conveyance is being used.

Forward Shipment: This type of contract covers actual commodities to be shipped at some future specified date.

Futures: A term used to designate any or all contracts covering the sale of commodities for future delivery made on an exchange and subject to its rules.

Grades: Various qualities according to accepted trade usage.

Grading Certificates: Certificates attesting to quality of a commodity graded by official inspectors, testers, graders, and so on.

Growths: Description of commodity according to area of growth; either refers to country, district, or place of semimanufacture.

GTC. Good till cancelled. Usually refers to open orders to buy or sell at a fixed price.

Hedge: A sale of any commodity for further delivery on or subject to the rules of any futures market to the extent that such sales are offset in quantity by the ownerships or purchase of the same cash commodity or, conversely, purchases of any commodity for future delivery on or subject to the rules of any futures market to the extent that such purchases are offset by sales of the same cash commodity.

Invisible Supply: Usually refers to uncounted stocks in hands of wholesalers, manufacturers, and ultimate consumers—sometimes to producers' stocks that cannot be accurately counted.

Life of Delivery: Period between first and last trade in any futures delivery contract.

Limited Order: An order given to a broker by a customer that has some restrictions upon its execution, such as price or time.

Liquidation: A transaction made in reducing or closing out a long or short position, but more often used by the trade to mean a reduction or closing out of a long position. (See "Cover.")

Loan Prices: The prices at which producers may obtain loans from the government for their crops.

Long: (1) The buying side of an open futures contract. (2) A trader whose net position in the futures market shows an excess of open purchases over open sales.

Lot: Usually any definite quantity of a commodity of uniform grade— (futures market)—the standard unit of trading.

Margin: Cash or equivalent posted as guarantee of fulfillment of a futures contract (not a part payment or purchase).

Margin Call: Demand for additional funds, or equivalent, because of adverse price movement or some other contingency.

Market Order: An order for immediate execution at the best available price.

Negotiable Warehouse Receipt: Document issued by warehouse, which guarantees existence and often specifies grade of commodity stored. Facilitates transfer of ownership by endorsement of receipt's owner.

Net Position: The difference between the open contracts long and the open contracts short held in any one commodity by any individual or group.

Nominal Price (Nominal quotation): Price quotations on a future and for a period in which no actual trading took place.

Offer: An offer, indicating willingness to sell at a given price. (Opposite of "Bid.")

On Opening: A term used to specify execution of an order during the opening.

Open Contracts: Contracts that have been bought or sold without the transaction having been completed by subsequent sale, or repurchase, or actual delivery or receipt of commodity.

Open Interest: The number of "open contracts." It refers to unliquidated purchases or sales and never to their combined total.

Open Order: An order that is good until cancelled.

Opening, The: The period at the beginning of the trading session officially designated by the exchange during which all transactions are considered made "at the opening."

Opening Price (or Range): The price (or price range) recorded during the period designated by the exchange as the official opening.

Pit: An octagonal platform on the trading floor of an exchange, consisting of steps upon which traders and brokers stand while executing futures trades. (See "Ring.")

Point: The minimum unit in which changes in futures price may be expressed. (Minimum price fluctuation may be in multiples of points.)

Position: An interest in the market in the form of open commitments.

Premium: The amount by which a given future or quality of a spot commodity sells over another future or quality of a spot commodity.

Price Limit: The maximum fluctuation in price of a futures contract permitted during one trading session, as fixed by the rules of a contract market.

Primary Markets: When used in connection with foreign-produced commodities, refers to country of production. In domestic commodities, refers to centers that receive commodities directly from country shippers.

Purchase and Sale Statement: A statement sent by a commission merchant to a customer when his or her futures position has been reduced to closed out. It shows the amount involved, the price at which the position was acquired and reduced or closed out, respectively, the gross profits or loss, the commission charged, and the net profit or loss, on the transaction. (Frequently referred to as a "P and S".)

Range: The difference between the high and low price of the future during a given period.

Reaction: The downward tendency of a commodity after an advance.

Realizing: When a profit is realized either by a liquidating sale or the repurchase of a short sale.

Resting Order: Instruction to buy or sell at figures away from the current level.

Ring: A circular platform on the trading floor of an exchange, consisting of steps upon which traders and brokers stand while executing futures trades. (See "Pit.")

Round Lot: The trading unit in which the major portion of trading occurs on those exchanges that make provisions for trading in two different units; prices of transactions in such units only are registered as official quotations.

Round Turn: The execution for the same principal of a purchase transaction and a sales transaction that offset each other.

Short: (1) The selling of an open futures contract. (2) A trader whose net position in the futures market shows all excess of open sales over open purchases. (See "Long.")

Spot Commodity: The actual physical commodity, as distinguished from the futures. (See "Cash commodity.")

Spot Price: The price at which the spot or cash commodity is selling. In grain trading it is called the "cash" price.

Stop Loss Order (or a Stop): Is one which becomes a market order only when the market reaches the level mentioned in the order. Its purpose is to limit losses. It may be either a buying order or a selling order. For example—"Sell Two October Cotton at 37.50 Stop." This indicates the person has bought at a price higher than 37.50 and wants to limit his or her loss to around the 37.50 level.

Straddle: Usually refers to purchase in one market and simultaneous sale of same commodity in some other market. May refer to purchase of one commodity against sale of a different commodity, both of which should normally be closely allied in price movements.

Switching: Simultaneously buying a contract for futures delivery in one month while selling a contract of the same commodity in another delivery month, on the same exchange.

Tenders: Issuance of transferable notices announcing intention of tendering or delivering actual commodity.

Transferable Notice: Notice given by the seller of a futures contract that he or she has made preparation for actual delivery.

Visible Supply: Usually refers to supplies of a commodity in recognized distribution centers, which have been moved from production areas to shipping centers. Varies with different commodities. Often includes afloats and all other supplies "in sight."

Volume of Trading (or Sales): Represents a simple addition of successive futures transactions. (A transaction consists of a purchase and matching sale.)

Wire House: A firm operating a private wire to its own branch offices, or to other firms.

Appendices

The reader is encouraged to make frequent use of the following appendices: an update on major commodities movements is included.

A schedule of commodities traded on the various exchanges along with margin requirements, trading limits, and contract sizes is also provided.

Armed with this additional information, the diligent commodities speculator is better prepared to devise an effective trading strategy.

APPENDIX 1. Commodity Futures Trading Information

COMMODITY TYPE	TRADING HOURS	CONTRACT SIZE	MINIMUM FLUCTUATION		DAILY LIMITS	
			PER UNIT	PER CONTRACT	PER UNIT	PER CONTRACT
Chicago Board of Trade						
Corn	9:30– 1:15	5,000 bu.	¼¢	12.50	10¢	$ 500.00
Oats	9:30– 1:15	5,000 bu.	¼¢	12.50	6¢	300.00
Soybeans	9:30– 1:15	5,000 bu.	¼¢	12.50	30¢	1,500.00
Soybean Meal	9:30– 1:15	100 short tonnes	10¢	10.00	10.00	1,000.00
Soybean Oil	9:30– 1:15	60,000 lbs.	1 pt.	6.00	1¢	600.00
Wheat	9:30– 1:15	5,000 bu.	¼¢	12.50	20¢	1,000.00
Plywood	9:00– 1:00	76,032 Sq. Ft.	10¢	7.60	$7.00	532.21
Iced Broilers	9:15– 1:20	30,000 lbs.	2½ pts.	7.50	200 pts.	600.00
(New) Gold	8:25– 1:35	100 troy oz.	10¢	10.00	$50.00	5,000.00
New Silver (1,000 oz.)	8:40– 1:25	1,000 troy oz.	10 pts.	10.00	40¢	400.00
Old Silver (5,000 oz.)	8:40– 1:25	5,000 troy oz.	10 pts.	50.00	40¢	2,000.00
Certificate Delivery GNMA	8:00– 2:00	$100,000.00	1/32	31/25	64/32	2,000.00
Ginnie Mae	8:00– 2:00	$100,000.00	1/32	31/25	64/32	2,000.00
Long-Term Treasury Bonds	8:00– 2:00	$100,000.00	1/32	31/25	64/32	2,000.00
4–6 Year Treasury Notes	8:00– 2:00	$100,000.00	1/32	31/25	64/32	2,000.00
30 Day Commercial Paper	8:30– 1:45	$3,000,000.00	1 pt.	25.00	50 pts.	1,250.00
90 Day Commercial Paper	8:30– 1:35	$1,000,000.00	1 pt.	25.00	50 pts.	1,250.00
Chicago Mercantile Exchange						
Feeder Cattle	9:05–12:45	42,000 lbs.	2½ pts.	10.50	1½¢	630.00
Live Cattle	9:05–12:45	40,000 lbs.	1½ pts.	10.00	1½¢	600.00
Live Hogs	9:10– 1:00	30,000 lbs.	2½ pts.	7.50	1½¢	450.00
Pork Bellies	9:10– 1:00	38,000 lbs.	2½ pts.	9.50	@¢	760.00
Eggs	9:20– 1:00	22,500 doz.	5 pts.	11.25	2¢	450.00
Lumber	9:00– 1:05	130,000 Bd. Ft.	10¢	13.00	5.00	650.00
Russet Burbank Potatoes	9:00– 1:00	80,000 lbs.	1 pt.	8.00	50¢	400.00

APPENDIX 1. Commodity Futures Trading Information (continued)

COMMODITY TYPE	TRADING HOURS	CONTRACT SIZE	MINIMUM FLUCTUATION		DAILY LIMITS	
			PER UNIT	PER CONTRACT	PER UNIT	PER CONTRACT
COMEX						
Copper	8:50— 1:00	25,000 lbs.	5 pts.	12.50	5¢	1,250.00
Gold	8:25— 1:30	100 troy oz.	10¢	10.00	25.00	2,500.00
Silver	8:40— 1:15	5,000 troy oz.	10 pts.	5.00	50¢	2,500.00
Zinc	8:00— 1:15	60,000 lbs.	5 pts.	30.00	3¢	1,800.00
International Monetary Market						
British Pound	7:30— 1:24	25,000 B.P.	5 pts.	$12.50	500 pts.	$1,250.00
Canadian Dollar	7:30— 1:22	100,000 D.C.	1 pt.	10.00	75 pts.	750.00
Deutschemark	7:30— 1:20	125,000 D.M.	1 pt.	12.50	100 pts.	1,250.00
Japanese Yen	7:30— 1:26	12,500,000 J.Y.	1 pt.	12.50	100 pts.	1,250.00
Mexican Peso	7:30— 1:18	1,000,000 M.P.	1 pt.	10.00	150 pts.	1,500.00
Swiss Franc	7:30— 1:16	125,000 S.F.	1 pt.	12.50	150 pts.	1,875.00
Gold	8:25— 1:30	100 troy oz.	10¢	10.00	$50.00	5,000.00
90 Day Treasury Bills	8:00— 1:40	$1,000,000.00	1 pt.	25.00	60 pts.	1,500.00
One Year U.S. Treasury Bills	8:15— 1:35	$250,000.00	1 pt.	25.00	50 pts.	1,250.00
Four Year Treasury Notes	8:20— 1:55	$1,000,000.00	$1/64$	15.62	$48/64$	750.00
Mid America Commodity Exchange						
Corn	9:30— 1:30	1,000 bu.	⅛¢	1.25	10¢	100.00
Oats	9:30— 1:30	5,000 bu.	⅛¢	6.25	6¢	300.00
Soybeans	9:30— 1:30	1,000 bu.	⅛¢	1.25	30¢	300.00
Wheat	9:30— 1:30	1,000 bu.	⅛¢	1.25	20¢	200.00
Live Cattle	9:05— 1:00	20,000 lbs.	2½ pts.	5.00	1½¢	300.00
Live Hogs	9:10— 1:15	15,000 lbs.	2½ pts.	3.75	1½¢	225.00
Gold	8:25— 1:40	33.2 troy oz.	10¢	3.32	$50.00	1,660.00
Silver	8:40— 1:40	1,000 troy oz.	10 pts.	10.00	40¢	400.00

New York Cocoa, Coffee & Sugar Exchange					
Cocoa	8:30— 2:00	10 metric tonnes	1 pt.	10.00	$88.00	880.00
Coffee	8:45— 1:30	37,500 lbs.	1 pt.	3.75	4¢	1,500.00
Sugar #11	9:00—12:45	112,000 lbs.	1 pt.	11.20	100 pts.	1,120.00
New York Cotton Exchange					
Cotton	9:30— 2:00	5,000 lbs.	1 pt.	5.00	2¢	1,000.00
Orange Juice	9:15— 1:45	15,000 lbs.	5 pts.	7.50	5¢	750.00
New York Mercantile Exchange					
Gold	8:25— 1:30	One kilo	20¢	6.40	$24.00	768.00
Gold	8:25— 1:30	400 troy oz.	5¢	20.00	$25.00	10,000.00
Platinum	8:30— 1:30	50 troy oz.	10¢	5.00	$20.00	1,000.00
Round White Potatoes	9:00— 1:00	5,000 lbs.	1 pt.	5.00	50 pts.	250.00
Heating Oil #2	9:30— 1:45	42,000 gal.	1 pt.	4.20	2¢	840.00
Fuel Oil #6	9:30— 1:45	42,000 gal.	1 pt.	4.20	2¢	840.00

UNITED STATES

	TRADING HOURS LOCAL TIME	CONTRACT UNIT	MINIMUM PRICE CHANGE PER UNIT	MINIMUM PRICE CHANGE PER CONTRACT	VALUE OF 1¢/$1 MOVE	MAXIMUM DAILY PRICE CHANGE	MAXIMUM DAILY PRICE RANGE	CONTRACT VALUE OF MAXIMUM MOVE	TRADING LIMIT NOTES
Imported Lean Beef NYMEX	10:15– 1:45	36,000 Lbs.	2¢ cwt	$ 7.20	$360.	$1.50	$3.00	$ 540.	$2 & $4 During Delivery Month
Broilers, Frozen Fresh CME	9:10– 1:00	30,000 Lbs.	2½¢ 100¢ Lb.	$ 7.50	$300.	2¢	4¢	600.	No Limit on Spot Month During Delivery Month
Cattle, Midwestern CME	9:05–12:45	40,000 Lbs.	2½¢ 100¢ Lb.	$10.00	$400.	1½¢	3¢	$600.	
Cattle, Midwestern MACE	9:05– 1:00	20,000 Lbs.	.00025¢ Lb.	$ 5.00	$200.	1½¢	3¢	$300.	
Citrus (FCOJ) NYCE	10:15– 2:45	15,000 Lbs.	5/100¢ Lb.	$ 7.50	$150.	5¢	10¢	$ 750.	No Limit on Spot Month On And After 8th Day
Cocoa NYCSC	9:30– 2:55	10 Metric Tons	$1 Metric Ton	$10.00	$ 10.	$88	$176.	$ 880.	No Limit On Spot Month On And After 8th Day
Coffee C NYCSC	9:45– 2:28	37,500 Lbs.	$1/100C Lb.	$ 3.75	$375.	4¢	8¢	$1500.	No Limit On Spot Month In Notice Period
Copper COMEX	9:50– 2:00	25,000 Lbs.	05/100¢ Lb.	$12.50	$250.	5¢	10¢	$1250.	No Limit On Spot On & After Day Prior to FND
Corn CBT	9:30– 1:15	5,000 Bus	¼¢ Bu	$12.50	$ 50.	10¢	20¢	$ 500.	
Corn MACE	9:30– 1:15	1,000 Bus	¼¢ Bu	$ 1.25	$ 10.	10¢	20¢	$ 100.	
Cotton NYCE	10:30– 3:00	10,000 Lbs.	$¹/₁₀₀¢ Lb.	$ 5.00	$500.	2¢	4¢	$1000.	No Limit On Spot Month On & After FND
Currencies, Foreign IMM									
British Pound	7:30– 1:24	25,000	.0005	$12.50		.05	.1000	$1200.	
Canadian Dollar	1:22	100,000	.0001	$10.00		.0075	.0150	$ 750.	
Deutschemark	1:20	125,000	.0001	$12.50		.01	.0200	$1250.	No Limit On Spot Month Beginning On Day Previous Month Expires
Dutch Guilder	1:30	125,000	.0001	$12.50		.01	.0200	$1250.	
French Franc	1:28	250,000	.0005	$12.50		.005	.010	$1250.	
Japanese Yen	1:26	12,500,000	.00001	$12.50		.0001	.0002	$1250.	
Mexican Peso	1:18	1,000,000	.00001	$12.50		.0015	.003	$1500.	

Commodity	Hours	Contract Size	Min. Fluctuation						Remarks
Swiss Franc	1:16	125,000	.0001	$12.50	$420.	.015	.03	$1875.	
Feeder Cattle CME	9:05–12:45	42,000 Lbs.	$.000025 Lb.	$10.50	$100.	1½¢	3¢	$ 630.	
Gold CBT	8:25– 1:35	100 Tr. Oz.	10¢ Oz.	$10.00	$100.	$40.00	$80.00	$4000.	No Limit On Spot Month During Delivery Month
Gold COMEX	9:25– 1:35	100 Tr. Oz.	10¢ Oz.	$10.00	$100.	$25.00	$50.00	$2500.	No Limit On Spot Month During Delivery Period
Gold IMM	8:25– 1:30	100 Tr. Oz.	10¢ Oz.	$10.00	$100.	$50.00	$100.00	$5000.	No Limit On Spot Month During Delivery Month
Gold MACE	8:25– 1:40	33.2 Tr Oz.	2.5¢ Oz.	$ .83	$33.20	$25.00	$50.00	$ 830.	No Limit On Spot Month During Delivery Month
GNMA CDR CBT	8:00– 2:00	$100,000	1/32 Pt.	$31.25	1 Pt= $1000	64/32nds	128/32nds	$2000.	No Limit On Spot Month During Delivery Period
GNMA CD CBT	8:00– 2:00	$100,000	1/32 Pt.	$31.25	1 Pt = $1000	64/32nds	128/32nds	$2000.	No Limit On Spot Month During Delivery Period
Hogs, Live CME	9:10– 1:00	30,000 Lbs.	2½ 100¢ Lb.	$ 7.50	$300.	1½¢	3¢	$ 450.	
Hog Live MACE	9:10– 1:15	15,000 Lbs.	.025¢ Lb.	$ 3.75	$150.	1½¢	3¢	$ 225.	
Lumber CME	9:00– 1:05	130,000 BD Ft	10¢ MBF	$13.00	$130.	$5.00	$10.00	$ 850.	
Lumber, Stud CME	9:00– 1:05	100,000 BD Ft	10¢ MBF	$10.00	$100.	$5.00	$10.00	$ 500.	
Oats CBT	9:30– 1:15	5,000 Bus	¼¢ Bu	$12.50	$ 50.	6¢	12¢	$ 300.	
Oats MACE	9:30– 1:30	5,000 Bus	⅛¢ Bu	$ 6.25	$ 50.	6¢	12¢	$ 300.	
#2 Heating Oil NYMEX	10:30– 2:45	42,000 US gas	$.0001 GAL	$ 4.20	$420.	2¢	4¢	$ 840.	Limit Off In Month Prior To Delivery Month
Palladium NYMEX	9:50– 2:20	100 Tr Oz.	5¢ Tr Oz	$ 5.00	$100.	$ 6.00	$12.00	$ 600.	No Limit On Last Trading Day
Platinum NYMEX	9:30– 2:30	50 Tr Oz.	10¢ Tr Oz.	$ 5.00	$ 50.	$20.00	$40.00	$1000.	No Limit On Last Trading Day
Plywood CBT	9:00– 1:00	76,032 Sq. Ft.	10¢ MSF	$ 7.60	$ 76.	$ 7.00	$14.00	$ 532.	No Limit On Spot Month On and After FND
Plywood, Western CBT	9:00– 1:00	76,032 Sq. Ft.	10¢ MSF	$ 7.60	$ 76.	$ 7.00	$14.00	$ 532.	
Pork Bellies	9:10– 1:00	38,000 Lbs.	$.00025 Lb.	$ 9.50	$380.	$ .02	$ .04	$ 760.	
Potatoes, Red White	10:00– 2:00	50,000 Lbs.	1¢ cwt.	$ 5.00	$ 5.	$ .50	$ 1.00	$ 250.	No Limit On LTD
Potatoes, Russet Burbank CME	9:00–12:50	80,000 Lbs.	1¢ cwt.	$ 8.00	$ 8.	$ .50	$ 1.00	$ 400.	$1 & $2 On LTD

COMMODITY AND EXCHANGE	TRADING HOURS LOCAL TIME	CONTRACT UNIT	MINIMUM PRICE CHANGE PER UNIT	MINIMUM PRICE CHANGE PER CONTRACT	VALUE OF 1¢/$1/L1 MOVE	MAXIMUM DAILY PRICE CHANGE	MAXIMUM DAILY PRICE RANGE
Lead-London LME	12:10–12:13, 12:45–12:50, 15:30–15:35, 16:00–16:05, 13:15–13:25, 16:40–17:00 (KERB)	25 Metric Tons	L25	L6.25 L25	None	None	
Nickel-London LME	12:20–12:25, 13:00–13:05, 15:45–15:50, 16:30–16:35, 13:15–13:25, 16:40–17:00 (KERB)	6 Metric Tons	L1 Tons	L6 L6	None	None	
Rubber-London Rubber Term Mkt Assoc.	8:45–09:30 Kerb, 9:45–12:45, 14:30–17:05	15 Tons (5 Tons Per Mo in 3 Mon Period)	0.10 Pence Kilo	L1.50 —	3 Pence	None	
Silver-London LME	11:50–11:55, 13:05–13:10, 15:50–15:55, 16:35–16:40, 13:15–13:25, 16:40–17:00 (KERB)	10,000 Troy Ounces	.05P Troy Ounces		None		
Soybean Meal-London Gafta Soyameal Fut Mkt	10:30–12:20, 14:30–17:00 Kerb After Official Call Until 19:15	100 Metric Tons (1000 Kilos Each)	L100 Tons	L10 L100		L500	
Sugar-London White Unit Term Sug Mkt Assoc	10:30–12:30, 14:30–17:00, 17:00–20:00, (KERB)	50 Metric Tons	L5 Tons	L25	L20	L40	No Limit On Spot Month
Sugar London Mkt Assoc Unit Term Sug Mkt Assoc	10:30–12:30, 14:30–17:00, 17:00–20:00, (KERB)	50 Metric Tons	L5 Tons	L25	L20	L40	No Limit On Spot Month
Sugar-London Raws #4 Unit Term Sug Mkt Assoc	10:30–12:30, 14:30–17:00, 17:00–20:00 (KERB)	50 Metric Tons	L5 Tons	L25	L20	L40	No Limit On Spot Month
Tin-London LME	Kerb 13:15, 13:25; 12:05–12:10, 12:40–12:45; Kerb 16:40, 17:00; 15:40–15:45, 16:20–16:25	5 Metric Tons	L1 Tons	L5	None	None	

COMMODITY AND EXCHANGE	TRADING HOURS LOCAL TIME	CONTRACT UNIT	MINIMUM PRICE CHANGE PER UNIT	PER CONTRACT	VALUE OF 1¢/$1/L1 MOVE	MAXIMUM DAILY PRICE CHANGE	PRICE RANGE
Zinc-London LME	12:15–12:20, 12:50–12:55, 15:30–15:35, 16:05–16:10, 13:15–13:25, 16:40–17:00 (KERB)	25 Metric Tons	L25 Tons	L6	None	None	None
Gas Oil In Bulk Intl Pet Ex of London	09:30–12:30, 02:45–05:20	100 Tons	25¢ US Tons	$25		$30	None

LONDON/SYDNEY

COMMODITY AND EXCHANGE	TRADING HOURS LOCAL TIME	CONTRACT UNIT	MINIMUM PRICE CHANGE PER UNIT	PER CONTRACT	VALUE OF 1¢/$1/L1 MOVE	MAXIMUM DAILY PRICE CHANGE	PRICE RANGE
Aluminum, London LME	Kerb 13:15–13:25, 11:55–12:00, 12:55–13:00, 15:45–15:50, 16:25–16:30	25 Metric Tons	L25	L25	L25	None	None
Cocoa-London Cocoa Terminal Mkt Assoc	10:00–13:00, 14:30–16:45	10 Metric (1,000 KGS)	L1 Tons	L10	L10	L40	None
Coffee London Robusta Coffee Term Mkt Assoc.	10:30–12:30, 14:30–17:00	5 Metric Tons	L1 Tons	L5	L5	None	None
Coffee No. 2 Arabica Coffee Term Mkt Assoc.	10:15–16:45	17,250 Kilos (250 Bags of 69 Kilos)	$.05 50 Kilos	$17.25	$3.45	None	None
Copper-High Grade LME	12:00–12:05, 12:30–12:35, 15:35–15:40, 16:10–16:15, 13:15–13:25, 16:40–17:00 (KERB)	25 Metric Tons	L5 Tons	L12.5	L25	None	None
Standard Copper-Catnodes LME	12:00–12:05, 16:15–16:20, 15:35–15:40, 16:15–16:20, 13:15–1325, 16:40–17:00 (KERB)	25 Metric Tons	L5 Tons	L12.5	L25	None	None

COMMODITY AND EXCHANGE	TRADING HOURS LOCAL TIME	CONTRACT UNIT	MINIMUM PRICE CHANGE PER UNIT	PER CONTRACT	VALUE OF 1¢/$1/L1 MOVE	MAXIMUM DAILY PRICE CHANGE	PRICE RANGE
Gold-London Bullion	08:30–19:30 Fixes Held At 10:30 AM 15:00 PM	Min. Order Outside of Fixes is 400 Ozs Min. Order for Fixes are 100 Ozs Min. order for Covering vs Amsterdam Mkt is 10 Ozs	NA	NA	NA	None	None
Silver-London Bullion	08:30–19:30 Fix held at 12:15	Min. Order is 5000 Ozs Min. Order for Daily Fix 1000 Ozs	NA	NA	NA	None	None
Crossbred, Greasy Wool #2 Ldn Wool Term Mkt Assoc	10:30–12:00, 15:00–16:30, Kerb Until 17:30	1500 Kilos	1 Pence Kilo				
Greasy Wool Sydney	11:00–12:30 15:00–16:30	1500 Kilos	.10¢ Per Kilo	$1.50 Aust			

CANADA

	TRADING HOURS (LOCAL TIME)	CONTRACT UNIT	MINIMUM PRICE CHANGE PER UNIT	PER CONTRACT	VALUE OF 1¢/$1 MOVE	MAXIMUM DAILY PRICE CHANGE	PRICE RANGE	CONTRACT VALUE OF MAXIMUM MOVE
Barley—Domestic Feed WGE	9:30–1:15	100 Tons (BD LOT) 20 Tons (JOB LOT)	10¢ Ton	$ 20.00 $100. CDN	$ 20. $100.	$ 5.00	$10.00	$ 100 $ 500.
Flaxseed WGE	9:30–1:15	100 Tons (ND LOT) 20 Tons (JOB LOT)	10¢ Ton	$ 20.00 $100. CDN	$ 20. $100.	$10.00	$20.00	$ 200 $1000.
Oats—Domestic Feed WGE	9:30–1:15	100 Tons (BD LOT) 20 Tons (JOB LOT)	10¢ Ton	$ 20.00 $100. CDN	$ 20. $100.	$ 5.00	$10.00	$ 200 $1000.
Rye WGE	9:30–1:15	100 Tons (BD LOT) 20 Tons (JOB LOT)	10¢ Ton	$ 20.00 $100. CDN	$ 20. $100.	$ 5.00	$10.00	$ 100 $5000.

COMMODITY AND EXCHANGE	TRADING HOURS LOCAL TIME	CONTRACT UNIT	MINIMUM PRICE CHANGE PER UNIT	PER CONTRACT	VALUE OF 1¢/$1/L1 MOVE	MAXIMUM DAILY PRICE CHANGE	PRICE RANGE	TRADING LIMIT NOTES
Rapseed—Vancouver WGE	9:30-1:15	100 Tons (BD LOT) 20 Tons (JOB LOT)	10¢ Ton	$ 20.00 $100. CDN	$ 20. $100.	$10.00	$20.00	$ 200 $1000.
Wheat—Domestic Feed WGE	9:30-1:15	100 Tons (BD LOT) 20 Tons (JOB LOT)	10¢ Ton	$ 20.00 $100. CDN	$ 20. $100.	$ 5.00	$10.00	$ 100. $1000.
Treasury Bills (90 Day) Toronto Stock Exchange	9:30-3:15	$1,000,000 Board Lot	1 Basis Pt. .01	$ 25.00 CDN	100 Basis Pts=$2500	60 Basis Pt. .60	120 Basis Pts 120	$1500.
Gold—Toronto	8:25-1:30	20 Ozs	10¢ Oz	$ 2.00	$ 20.00	$30.00	$ .60	$ 600.
Silver—Toronto	8:40-1:25	200 Ozs	1¢ Oz	$ 2.00	$ 2.00	50¢	$ 1.00	$ 100.
Treasury Bonds TSE	9:30-3:15	$1000,000 at 9%	$31.25	$ 31.25	$32nd $1000	$^{64}/34nds	$^{128}/32nds	$2000

HONG KONG/KUALA LUMPUR

COMMODITY AND EXCHANGE	TRADING HOURS LOCAL TIME	CONTRACT UNIT	MINIMUM PRICE CHANGE PER UNIT	PER CONTRACT	VALUE OF 1¢/$1/L1 MOVE	MAXIMUM DAILY PRICE CHANGE	PRICE RANGE	TRADING LIMIT NOTES
Cotton Hong Kong Cmdy Ex	9:45-11:15 15:00-16:30	50,000 LBs	$^{1}/_{100}$¢ US Lb	$ 5.00				
Soybeans Hong Kong	4 Sessions 9:50 AM, 10:50 AM, 12:50 PM, 02:50 PM	500 Bags of 60 Kgs	20HK¢					
Sugar Hong Kong	10:15-11:45 14:30-16:00	50 Long Tons (112,000 LBs)	$^{1}/_{100}$¢ US	$11.20				
Gold Hong Kong	9:00-12:00 14:30-17:30	100 Tr Oz	10¢ US 10¢ US	$10.00				
Palm Oil—Kuala Lumpur Kuala Lumpur Cmdy Ex	11:00-12:30 3:00- 6:00	25 Metric Tons	$1 Malaysia	$25.00 Malaysia		1st day—$ 5.00 2nd day—$ 75.00 3rd day—$100.00 4th day—None 5th day—$ 50.00		

	DAY	OVERNIGHT
Chicago Board of Trade		
Corn	50.00	65.00
Oats	50.00	65.00
Soybeans	50.00	65.00
Soybean Meal	50.00	65.00
Soybean Oil	50.00	65.00
Wheat	50.00	65.00
Iced Broilers	50.00	65.00
Plywood	50.00	65.00
Gold	50.00	65.00
Silver (5,000 troy oz.)	50.00	65.00
Silver (1,000 troy oz.)	30.00	35.00
Long-Term Treasury Bonds	55.00	80.00
Certificate of Deposit	55.00	80.00
Ginnie Mae	55.00	80.00
Certificate Delivery GNMA	55.00	80.00
4–6 Year Treasury Notes	55.00	80.00
30 Day Commercial Paper	55.00	80.00
90 Day Commercial Paper	55.00	80.00
Chicago Mercantile Exchange		
Feeder Cattle	50.00	65.00
Live Cattle	50.00	65.00
Live Hogs	50.00	65.00
Pork Bellies	50.00	65.00
Eggs	50.00	65.00
Lumber	50.00	65.00
Russet Burbank Potatoes	50.00	65.00
COMEX		
Copper	60.00	75.00
Gold	70.00	95.00
Silver	60.00	85.00
International Monetary Market		
Currencies	50.00	70.00
Gold	50.00	70.00
Silver Coins	50.00	70.00
90 Day Treasury Bills	50.00	70.00
1 Year Treasury Bills	50.00	70.00
Certificate of Deposit	50.00	70.00
4 Year Treasury Notes	50.00	70.00
Kansas City Board of Trade		
Wheat	45.00	50.00

	DAY	OVERNIGHT
Mid America Commodity Exchange		
Corn	25.00	30.00
Oats	25.00	30.00
Soybeans	25.00	30.00
Wheat	25.00	30.00
Live Cattle	30.00	35.00
Live Hogs	30.00	35.00
Gold	35.00	40.00
Silver	35.00	40.00
New York Cocoa, Coffee & Sugar Exchange		
Cocoa	60.00	85.00
Coffee	60.00	90.00
Sugar	60.00	85.00
New York Cotton Exchange		
Cotton	60.00	80.00
Orange Juice	60.00	80.00
New York Mercantile Exchange		
Gold	70.00	95.00
Platinum	50.00	65.00
Silver Coins	60.00	85.00
Heating Oil & Fuel Oil	50.00	60.00
Round White Potatoes	50.00	60.00

APPENDIX 3. Margin Requirements—Cash Deposit Required

COMMODITY	OUTRIGHT		SPREAD		SPOT MONTH	
	INITIAL	MAINTENANCE	INITIAL	MAINTENANCE	OUTRIGHT	SPREAD
Wheat (5M bu.)	1,000.00	750.00	250.00	250.00	25,000.00	12,500.00
Wheat (1M bu.)	200.00	150.00	10.00	10.00	5,000.00	2,500.00
Corn (5M bu.)	600.00	500.00	125.00	125.00	20,000.00	10,000.00
Corn (1M bu.)	100.00	60.00	10.00	10.00	4,000.00	2,000.00
Soybeans (5M bu.)	1,500.00	1,000.00	500.00	500.00	40,000.00	20,000.00
Soybeans (1M bu.)	300.00	200.00	20.00	20.00	8,000.00	4,000.00
Oats (5M bu.)	400.00	300.00	75.00	75.00	12,500.00	6,250.00
Oats (1M bu.)	60.00	40.00	10.00	10.00	2,500.00	1,250.00
Soybean Oil	600.00	400.00	150.00	150.00	15,000.00	10,000.00
Soybean Meal	1,000.00	600.00	225.00	225.00	25,000.00	25,000.00
Kansas City Wheat	1,000.00	600.00	100.00	100.00	4,500.00	1,000.00
Kansas City Chicago Wheat			500.00	500.00		
Silver (5M oz. CMX)	3,000.00	2,250.00	330.00	248.00	50,000.00	50,000.00
(5M oz. BOT)	3,500.00	2,500.00	200.00	200.00	12,500.00	10,000.00
(1M oz. BOT)	700.00	500.00	100.00	100.00		
(1M oz. MACE)	500.00	375.00	50.00	50.00	10,000.00	5,000.00
Gold (100 oz. COMEX)	1,500.00	1,125.00	320.00	240.00	20,000.00	20,000.00
(100 oz. IMM)	2,000.00	1,500.00	200.00	200.00	20,000.00	20,000.00
(33.2 oz. MACE)	600.00	400.00	50.00	50.00	12,500.00	10,000.00
New Gold (100 oz. BOT)	2,500.00	1,000.00	200.00	200.00	20,000.00	20,000.00
Platinum	1,000.00	700.00	200.00	140.00	6,000.00	1,300.00
Copper	900.00	675.00	130.00	98.00	5,000.00	2,000.00
Iced Broilers	500.00	400.00	100.00	100.00	5,000.00	1,000.00
Pork Bellies	1,200.00	900.00	700.00	400.00	19,000.00	10,000.00
Live Cattle (CME)	900.00	600.00	400.00	200.00	36,000.00	
Live Cattle (MACE)	450.00	300.00	100.00	100.00	12,000.00	10,000.00
Feeder Cattle	900.00	600.00	400.00	200.00	25,000.00	15,000.00

Live Hogs (CME)	700.00	500.00	300.00	15,000.00	75,000.00
Live Hogs (MACE)	360.00	240.00	120.00	8,000.00	3,000.00
Eggs	700.00	600.00	500.00	14,500.00	5,000.00
Russet Burbank Potatoes	500.00	350.00	175.00	5,000.00	3,500.00
Round White Potatoes	500.00	350.00	175.00	5,000.00	3,500.00
Plywood	700.00	400.00	200.00	4,000.00	800.00
Lumber	1,200.00	800.00	400.00	6,000.00	1,200.00
Orange Juice	1,000.00	750.00	188.00	21,000.00	10,000.00
Cotton	1,500.00	1,125.00	563.00	5,000.00	1,000.00
Coffee	5,500.00	4,125.00	1,125.00	45,000.00	25,000.00
Cocoa	2,000.00	1,500.00	338.00	9,500.00	4,800.00
Sugar #11	2,500.00	1,875.00	1,313.00	10,000.00	9,000.00
Heating Oil	2,000.00	1,400.00	140.00		
GNMA—CD	2,000.00	1,500.00	200.00	3,000.00	1,000.00
Ginnie Mae	2,000.00	1,500.00	200.00	3,000.00	1,000.00
U.S. Treasury Bonds BOT	2,000.00	1,500.00	200.00	3,000.00	1,000.00
Treasury Bonds MACE	1,000.00	750.00	100.00		
90 Day Treasury Bills	2,000.00	1,500.00	200.00	3,000.00	1,000.00
One Year Treasury Bills	1,000.00	700.00	200.00	3,000.00	1,000.00
CD (BOT)	2,000.00	1,500.00	400.00	2,000.00	400.00
CD (IMM)	1,500.00	1,200.00	200.00	1,500.00	300.00
Treasury Bills CD (IMM)	500.00	400.00	300.00		
Commercial Paper	1,500.00	1,200.00	200.00	3,000.00	1,000.00
Treas. BD/CD (BOT)	1,200.00				
British Pound	1,500.00	1,000.00	400.00	13,000.00	2,000.00
Canadian Dollar	1,200.00	900.00	400.00	15,000.00	2,500.00
Deutschemark	1,500.00	1,000.00	400.00	13,000.00	2,000.00
Japanese Yen	1,500.00	1,000.00	400.00	13,000.00	2,000.00
Mexican Peso	4,000.00	3,000.00	2,000.00	15,000.00	2,500.00
Swiss Franc	2,000.00	1,500.00	400.00	15,000.00	2,500.00

APPENDIX 4.
ANALYSIS OF COMMODITY PRICES: COFFEE, COCOA, SUGAR, AND COPPER

Summary

This memorandum analyzes the general outlook for commodity prices and presents price forecasts for coffee, cocoa, sugar, and copper under two scenarios.

Commodity prices were likely to remain weak in 1982. The world-wide recessionary environment lowered demand at a time when abundant supplies, both from rising production and large stocks, were anticipated. Due to a tight monetary policy, interest rates in the United States were still unusually high, holding back the economic recovery and adding to the downward pressure on commodity prices. Lower energy prices brought world inflation rates down faster than anticipated, and as inflation continued to unwind, the general outlook for commodity prices necessarily became more bearish. With prices falling below agreed floors, commodity agreements were not expected to influence the market.

In our forecast of August 1981, we considered two different scenarios: pessimistic and most likely. In general, conditions assumed under the pessimistic case materialized. For example, a weaker-than-anticipated world economy emerged, and higher-than-expected U.S. interest rates persisted.

Given the changed world economic setting (slower growth and lower energy prices and inflation) as well as the possibility that the U.S. economy may be entering a phase of disinflation, the general commodity price outlook for 1983 and beyond has turned bearish relative to prior expectations. While in our previous forecast we expected prices to be rising in 1983 with a bull market for commodities occurring in 1984, we now expect commodity prices to remain weak for a much longer period and with less pronounced price rises.

In 1981–1982, the IMF index of commodity prices fell 15 percent from its 1980 average level and some 40 percent from its high in early 1980. The two-year decline in prices was due to demand/supply developments. On the demand side, recessionary conditions worldwide slowed world trade while high interest rates and a strong U.S. dollar discouraged consumers and speculators from replenishing or holding inventories. As for supply, despite surpluses generated from expansion plans during the last commodity boom, many developing country-producers, hard pressed for foreign exchange to service their external debts, did not restrain production. Hence, sustained increases in supply in face of sluggish demand caused stocks to rise and prices to fall.

Two possible cases are considered in this commodity analysis: most likely and pessimistic. The assumptions for each case follow.

Most Likely Case

World economic growth will be restrained by a subdued U.S. recovery. High and volatile interest rates will continue to discourage holding of inventories. Inflation slows further with the easing of oil prices.

Pessimistic Case

World economic growth is slower than forecast in the most likely case. A number of producing LDCs will push exports aggressively for two reasons: need for foreign exchange and warehousing problems.

Our commodity price forecast follows:

COMMODITY PRICE FORECAST

	Actual	Most Likely				Pessimistic			
	1981	1982	1983	1984	1985	1982	1983	1984	1985
Coffee	127	130	140	150	160	120	105	115	125
Cocoa	90	75	80	88	95	70	70	82	90
Sugar	17	10	15	17	20	9	8	12	15
Copper	79	68	78	90	110	65	70	80	88

Commodity prices during and after the two recessions, as well as the most recent prices available, are presented in the table below.

AVERAGE COMMODITY PRICES
(U.S. cents per pound)

	1973	1974†	1975†	1976	1977	1978	1979	1980†	1981†	July 1982
Coffee*	69	73	83	150	308	166	174	164	127	140
Cocoa	64	98	75	110	172	154	149	118	90	65
Sugar	10	30	20	12	8	8	10	29	17	8
Copper	81	93	56	64	59	62	90	99	79	65
IPI**	71	87	100	102	111	131	150	166	157	
(1975 = 100)										

*Brazilian coffee price series changed from ex Brazil to fob New York.
† Recession years.
**World Bank International Price Index.

COFFEE

Coffee prices in 1982 were expected to fall further from their mid-year levels but averaged somewhat higher than 1981's. The 1981–1982 coffee crop, a record at 96.6 million bags, provided a surplus to cover the projected loss in Brazil's frost-damaged 1982–1983 crop. With world demand expected to remain sluggish at 82 to 83 million bags, stocks at the end of the 1982–1983 season will still be large enough to cover 50 percent of annual consumption. Under our most likely forecast, we anticipate Brazil's coffee trees to recover slowly from the frost, allowing supply and demand to move more into balance over the next several years. Prices in 1982 were expected to fluctuate within the International Coffee Agreement's price range of $1.15 to $1.45 and average $1.30 a pound compared to $1.27 in 1981. In real terms, coffee prices over the next few years are likely to remain at their current low levels with nominal prices rising with the inflation rate up to 1985. Our pessimistic forecast assumes a faster recovery in Brazilian output and stagnant if not declining world demand, leading to accelerated stock accumulation and lower prices than under the most likely case.

COCOA

Cocoa prices will continue to be under pressure from excess supplies and are expected to remain weak despite buffer stock buying operations. Production has been exceeding demand for the past four years, and the outlook for the next several years is a continuation of this imbalance. Large cocoa crops through 1984–1985 will be coming from the Ivory Coast, Brazil, and Malaysia as new plantings bear fruit, mature, and achieve maximum yields. Consumption will continue to be buoyant due to relatively lower cocoa and sugar prices but will still lag behind production. Stocks, therefore, will rise to their highest level in years. Under both the most likely and the pessimistic forecasts, we were expecting cocoa prices in 1982 to remain way below the International Cocoa Agreement's intervention price of $1.10 a pound. Cocoa prices in 1982 were expected to average 70 to 75 cents a pound.

SUGAR

Sugar prices in 1982 were likely to stay relatively low compared to 1981's levels. Despite a healthy increase in consumption due to abundant supplies and lower prices, production in 1982 outpaced demand for the first time in three years—by as much as 4 percent or 4 million tons. This is because of expanded worldwide production, especially in the European Community region, resulting in a record 1981–1982 crop of 96 million tons—up 10 percent from 1981's output. Stocks at the end of the current season will rise to 27% of annual consumption. The outlook for the next few years, however, could very well change from oversupply to a more balanced supply-demand situation if sugar beet producers, both in the European Community region and the United States, carry out their intentions to cut back production. Unlike sugarcane, sugar beet is an annual crop, and changes in production this year can easily affect next year's supply. Under our most likely forecast, we anticipate a cutback in production and a strengthening of prices from 1983 to 1985. Sugar prices in 1982 were expected to average 10 cents a pound. Our pessimistic forecast assumes a delayed response from beet producers and a further weakening of prices in 1983 before improving in 1984–1985.

COPPER

The plunge in copper prices has been extraordinarily steep. We had anticipated a weak copper market in 1982, but the dismal performance far exceeded our prior gloomy expectations, with copper on the London Metal Exchange (LME) averaging a painfully low 59 cents a pound in June 1982. All of the worst things have happened: The United States has been in a severe recession, interest rates have remained relatively high, and foreign producers have generally not restricted production. The only positive development is that visible inventories are still quite low compared to 1976 and 1977 levels, though stocks are rising.

Some firming in price is likely to be evident as economic recovery in the United States takes hold. Nevertheless, the improvement in price will be relatively slow since the U.S. recovery is expected to be subdued and since non-U.S. producers—with Canada a notable exception—are generally not restraining output. We still expect the copper market to tighten by 1985, but the general level of prices is now expected to be dramatically lower than in our prior forecasts. Copper prices have already dropped to extraordinarily low levels, and the Federal Reserve has proved to be more resolute in its anti-inflation stance than had been previously anticipated.

Copper prices on the LME were expected to average 65–68 cents a pound in 1982 and 70–78 cents in 1983. By 1985, the most likely and pessimistic forecasts show substantial divergence, with copper at $1.10 under the most likely forecast and at 88 cents under the pessimistic scenario, which assumes prices remain depressed under the load of unrestrained LDC production, even though industrialized nations experience economic recovery.

COFFEE

World Demand

The prospects for increasing coffee consumption worldwide are poor. In the United States, the demand for coffee has been declining since 1976, and efforts to reverse the trend have been unsuccessful so far. The results of the 1981 Winter Coffee Drinking Survey undertaken by the International Coffee Organization indicated that although coffee remains the most popular beverage in the U.S., consumption per capita in 1981 declined by 5 percent. The chief reasons cited are the general consumer concern over caffeine as a health risk and competition from other beverages. In Western Europe, consumption appears to have stabilized in recent years after a long period of increases. Since population growth in these countries is expected to remain near zero, future coffee demand will depend mainly on growth in per capita income. The current low income growth among these nations means stagnant demand.

The brighter prospects for increased coffee drinking could come from Japan, the USSR, and the centrally-planned economies of Europe. However, these areas account for less than 15 percent of total world demand. Also, Eastern European imports are subject to foreign exchange constraints. For example, due to shortage of foreign exchange in Poland, 1982 coffee imports were restricted to 20,000 tons, down from the 1981 level of 36,000 tons. Producing countries, ideally, should offer the greatest potential growth, but consumption trends so far have been volatile with no clear pattern of future growth. This is probably because demand in producing countries is more or less dependent on government policies and prices.

Following a 3.5 percent decline in 1979–1980, world coffee demand in 1980–1981 stabilized somewhat at 81 million bags. Under our most likely forecast, we were expecting demand in 1981–1982 to at least equal the projected 1 percent growth of the world economy. This would be raising consumption to 82 million bags in 1981–1982. The pessimistic view is for demand to be flat at best or continue to decline because of weak world economic conditions.

World Production

The world coffee crop in 1981–1982 (October–September) was record large at 96.6 million bags. Brazil accounted for most of the increase as millions of its trees planted after the 1975 frost came of bearing age and produced a bumper crop of 32.5 million bags. This was 50 percent larger than the previous year's output. When world production is matched against projected world demand of about 82.3 million bags, some 15 million bags were to be added to stocks during 1982. However, because of the frosts in 1981, the Brazilian 1982–1983 crop is expected to be reduced to about 18 million bags. The surplus production this year will be large enough to offset the projected loss; hence, during 1982–1983, supply and demand will largely be in balance.

Beginning in 1983–1984, the amount of surplus production will generally depend on the policies of important coffee producers. Brazil's dependence on coffee exports is much less now than in the 1970's, but coffee production is more impressive than ever. There is no indication that Brazil will cut back its coffee output. Colombia is pushing for development of non-coffee sectors to be able to sustain the ups and downs of coffee prices. However, it has no intention of reducing its present world market share. Indonesia has abandoned plans to increase coffee-growing acreage but is bent on the rehabilitation of areas already under cultivation and on improvement of quality. Based on 1976 plantings, output could still increase 5 percent to 10 percent above the 1981–1982 crop. The Ivory Coast is discouraging further growth in production but will maintain current output. It plans to offer bonus payments to growers who offer high quality beans. Due to political and economic problems in the Central American countries, coffee production is forecast to decline near term, but almost all of these areas carry ample stocks to offset production shortfalls.

Given no visible crop-cutting programs in any of the large producing countries, surplus production over the next five years will therefore depend on how fast the Brazilian trees recover. Our most likely forecast assumes a steady but slow Brazilian recovery, allowing demand and supply to move more into balance. However, surplus stocks will remain large. A pessimistic view assumes a fast Brazilian recovery and an acceleration in the accumulation of coffee stocks, probably to the high levels of the 1960s.

Prices

On a monthly average basis, the New York spot price for Brazilian coffee peaked in February 1980 at $1.94 a pound. Thereafter, bumper crop prospects through 1982 and falling demand caused coffee prices to decline until June 1981, when they averaged $1.17 a pound or some 40 percent lower. In June 1981 the ICO Indicator Price fell below 90 cents a pound, and coffee futures dropped to 82 cents. In July 1981, Brazil suffered a frost, which was followed by a dry weather spell in August.

Speculation on crop damage pushed prices up temporarily, but when it became apparent that the crop loss would merely diminish the large accumulation of stocks, prices retreated lower to $1.14 a pound in September 1981. From October to December 1981, coffee prices improved and averaged $1.40 a pound, some 23 percent higher than the September level. Some analysts attributed the price improvement to the International Coffee Agreement's quota limitations, which went into effect in October 1981. In retrospect, the price improvement is the result of a number of developments but was not expected to be sustained during most of 1982.

First, as the ICO-imposed export quotas went into effect for the first quarter of the 1981–1982 crop-year (October to December 1981), the supply made available to ICO importing members was limited to a very restrictive amount (13 million bags) at a time when imports were seasonally heavy and roasters' stocks lean due to high interest rates. Second, producing members were somehow able to discipline themselves by keeping their surplus beans off the ICO market. Third, the

July 1981 frost which diminished the crop for the ensuing year probably reduced pressure to sell in anticipation of better market conditions.

Coffee prices averaged $1.27 a pound in 1981, down from their 1980 level of $1.64 a pound and 60 percent lower than their 1977 record price of $2.67 a pound. In 1982 coffee averaged $1.40 in January and $1.47 in February, and $1.38 a pound in July, down from a high of $1.54 in mid-February. As the purchasing period of roasters wound down, coffee prices were expected to decline further; hence, in 1982, coffee prices were expected to average $1.30 a pound.

The International Coffee Agreement

The ICA basically hopes to stabilize world coffee prices between $1.15 and $1.45 a pound by reducing quotas on exports when prices fall below the floor price of the agreement.

The agreement appeared to have had some influence on the market late in 1981. In the long run, it is doubtful if it could withstand pressures of accumulating surpluses. Stocks retained in producing countries have been increasing because of the disparity between production and ICA quotas. Brazil and Colombia may be able to stockpile surpluses, but a number of African producers, including the Ivory Coast, do not have the necessary warehouse facilities. Their need for foreign exchange will make them aggressive exporters despite declining prices. A lot of the surplus stock is now being sold to non-quota markets at lower prices, creating a two-tier price system for coffee export—one for member countries and another for non-member countries.

COCOA

World Demand

Despite relatively lower cocoa and sugar prices, a more rapid expansion of cocoa consumption was not likely to be achieved in 1982. Cocoa is consumed mostly by countries of relatively high income, and the continuing recessionary conditions in most of these countries, as well as the widespread use of cocoa substitutes and extenders, will restrain consumption growth. Nevertheless, cocoa use in 1981 was quite impressive, up 5.6 percent and surpassing the peak demand in 1971–1972. This means demand had fully recovered from its decline in 1976–1977 when prices soared.

For the next several years, demand is forecast to grow by 2.5 percent per annum. Under our most likely forecast we expect world demand to be stimulated by lower prices but still to lag behind production. Our pessimistic view sees demand growing at a much slower rate due to continued poor world economic conditions.

World Production

A record world cocoa crop was again harvested in 1981–1982 (October–September) with stocks increasing for the fifth consecutive year. On top of this, the outlook for the next several years is for large world crops as new plantings in major producing countries come into production and increase in productivity.

In the Ivory Coast, the 1980–1981 harvest of 412,000 tons came from only two-thirds of planted trees. One-third has not matured, and production by the mid-1980's is expected to approximate 500,000 tons, which would be 21 percent larger than the 1980–1981 crop. In Brazil, despite the slowdown in the expansion program, new plantings made during the past years will keep Brazilian production in a rising trend at least through 1985. In Malaysia, production is expected to rise sharply over the next several years as new plantings come into bearing and young trees increase in productivity. By 1985, the country is expected to be producing about 150,000 metric tons compared to the 1981–1982 crop of 60,000 tons.

Prices

On a monthly average basis, cocoa prices peaked in February 1980 at $1.42 a pound and hit a five-year low in June 1981, when they fell to 70 cents a pound. For the next six months, prices fluctuated from 88 cents to $1.01 with December prices averaging 92 cents. For the year 1981, cocoa prices averaged 90 cents a pound, down from $1.13 in 1980. In January 1982, cocoa averaged 96 cents; in February, 90 cents, and in March, 85 cents. July 1982 quotes were down to 65 cents a pound.

More than 100,000 metric tons of cocoa have already been taken off the market through Buffer stock operations. Another 30,000 to 50,000 tons are scheduled to be purchased by the Buffer Stock Fund with the $75 million loan from the Brazilian Bank consortium. Also, the Cocoa Producers Alliance, which includes as members major cocoa producing countries, has announced its intention to stockpile about 60,000 tons of the 1982–1983 crop, which we project will provide a surplus of about 80,000 tons. Against this, however, should be weighed the bearish prospect of stock rotation in the summer. Unlike coffee, cocoa cannot be stored for a long period of time; to maintain the quality of beans, stocks need to be swapped with new crops. In 1981, stock swapping had a bearish effect on prices.

International Cocoa Agreement

Despite the absence of the Ivory Coast (the largest producer) and the United States (the largest consumer) as members, the International Cocoa Agreement (ICCA) was provisionally implemented on August 1, 1981. The ICCA's objective was to try to stabilize cocoa bean prices between $1.10 and $1.50 per pound through a buffer stock scheme. At the time it was implemented, the Buffer Stock Fund (BSF) accumulated under earlier agreements amounted to $230 million. The BSF is authorized to purchase cocoa beans of up to 250,000 tons, which was some 40 percent of world stocks in 1981. By mid-1982, the BSF had purchased a total of 100,345 metric tons of cocoa beans.

From the start, the cocoa agreement's effectiveness has been questioned. It attempts to support prices at too high a level. Cocoa prices are quoted under $1.00 a pound, compared to the agreement's intervention price range of $1.15 to $1.50. The Buffer Stock Fund is not sufficient to finance maximum buffer stock operations. Its stock rotation procedure pushed prices lower instead of supporting them. For all its failings, however, it could probably be said that, without market anticipation of higher prices once buffer stock operations started, prices could have been more depressed.

SUGAR

World Demand

Sugar consumption in 1981 was down 1.2 percent following two seasons of static demand. In 1982, because of lower world prices as a result of abundant supplies, the anticipated increase was 4 percent. Over the next several years, much slower growth is being projected due to a number of factors. Consumption in most industrialized countries has reached a saturation point. In the United States and Japan, there have been significant declines because of higher use of high fructose corn syrup. Also, for dietary reasons and dental hygiene, per capita sugar consumption in the U.S. has been declining for years—from 102.8 pounds a year in 1973 to 85.6 in 1980. The increase in growth, therefore, will come primarily from developing countries due to their high population growth rates and—one hopes—rising standards of living.

Under our most likely forecast, we anticipate sugar use to continue to increase, although at a much reduced rate. Our pessimistic view assumes no growth in consumption.

World Production

World sugar production in 1981–1982 (September–August) outpaced demand for the first time in three years, by as much as 4 million metric tons. Bumper crops of both cane and beet sugar due to expanded world production increased world output by more than 10 percent to reach a record 96 million metric tons. Demand, after declining 1.2 percent in 1981, was projected to rise 4 percent in 1982, to 92 million metric tons. Hence, the production surplus of 4 million tons boosted stocks to 25 million tons or 27 percent of annual consumption.

Prices

World sugar prices peaked in October 1980 at 41 cents a pound and by September 1981 fell to 12 cents a pound—a 70 percent decline in eleven months. On a yearly basis, sugar prices in 1981 averaged 17 cents or 40 percent lower than their 1980 average of 29 cents a pound. With the record crop that was anticipated in 1981–1982, prices fluctuated close to the 12 to 13 cent range from October 1981 onward, but were about 8 cents a pound in July 1982.

International Sugar Agreement

The International Sugar Agreement was extended for two years beginning December 1982. The European Community is still not a member but is negotiating changes in certain provisions of the Agreement. The ISA hopes to stabilize sugar prices at a price range of 13 to 23 cents a pound through the use of quotas and buffer stocks. The efforts of the ISA to hold prices within the target range were unsuccessful both when they were rising in 1980 and when they were falling in 1981.

COPPER

Demand

Copper prices have been clobbered by high interest rates, which have produced a major recession in the United States, a worldwide economic slowdown, and—because copper demand is highly dependent on interest-rate sensitive industries—a sharp drop in the demand for copper. For example, even in 1981—a particularly bad year for the housing industry in the United States—copper used in building construction accounted for 29.0 percent of total United States copper production, the largest share among major categories, while 11.0 percent of copper production was used in transportation equipment. Industrial machinery, another highly cyclical industry, is also a major market for copper, accounting for 19.1 percent of demand in 1981. Copper's strong dependence on these markets underscores the sensitivity of short-run copper demand to interest rates and general economic fluctuations.

On a longer-term basis, the most rapid growth in copper consumption has been in developing nations trying to build their infrastructure. For example, refined copper consumption in South America, Africa, and Asia (excluding Japan) combined increased at an average annual rate of 7.8 percent from 1973 to 1981. In contrast, United States copper consumption in 1981 was 14.0 percent below the 1978 level, the most recent peak year, which in turn was slightly below the 1973 level. Although copper demand has been stagnant in the United States, it is still by far the world's largest consumer of copper.

The steep 15.9 percent decline in non-COMECON refined copper consumption in 1975 played a significant role in the extended bear market for copper that prevailed for several years thereafter. Consumption declined only 2.8 percent in 1980 and 2.3 percent in 1981 but was likely to decline more sharply—about 6 percent to 7 percent—in 1982. United States refined copper consumption declined 8.5 percent from first quarter 1981 to first quarter 1982, but some improvement was expected as economic recovery took hold in the second half of 1982.

Production and Inventories

Copper prices have fallen so low that they are now below production costs, not just in the United States but in low-cost areas, such as Chile, as well. In response, severe production cutbacks have been instituted in the United States and Canada. Phelps Dodge, the second largest United States producer, had closed all of its domestic copper mines since April 17, 1982, and had registered substantial losses, as have other producers. Such dramatic cutbacks would be expected to help prop up prices, except that most of the major producing countries other than the United States and Canada have made no attempt whatsoever to restrain production.

In assessing the current situation, one inevitably arrives at a sense of *déjà vu*. As in the period 1975–1978, LDCs under pressure to acquire foreign exchange to service their heavy burdens of external debt are not curtailing output even though prices are extraordinarily depressed. Three factors are different today, however. First, prices in real terms are even more depressed now than then, to the point that some spokesmen for LDCs have at least publicly questioned whether their interest would be best served by restraining production. Second, U.S. and Canadian producers have been quicker and more aggressive this time in shutting in production. The situation has become serious enough that—if the market does not improve—a significant portion of the United States copper industry may not survive in its present form. Third, high real interest rates for the last few years have acted as a strong disincentive to holding inventories. The latter point is crucial, since the huge buildup in stocks in 1976 and 1977 was the major depressant on copper prices during that period.

Copper inventories are indeed rising now, but to a much lesser degree than in 1976 and 1977. For example, copper stocks on the LME amounted to 706,800 short tons at year-end 1977. In contrast, LME inventories of copper were 139,600 tons at the end of 1981 and only 140,000 tons in mid-July 1982. Stocks at United States refiners, however, went from 62,200 tons in April 1981 to 220,000 tons in April 1982.

Total world stocks will probably continue to rise throughout 1982 and well into 1983 since most of the LDCs that are major producers of copper evidently lack the discipline to restrain production. Production cutbacks are being considered by Cipec (Intergovernmental Council of Copper Exporting Countries), of which Chile, Peru, Indonesia, Zaire, and Zambia are full members, but no palpable results are likely from any Cipec resolution.

Prices

The outlook for copper prices appears to be decidedly bearish through 1983, though prices will remain above the recent lows of about 60 cents a pound. The expected economic recovery in the United States will help limit the buildup in stocks and lend some support to prices, but a continued rise in world inventories seems inevitable for another year or so given the continued high levels of production in the LDCs. It is quite likely, however, that at least one temporary rally will be evident during this period. United States consumers of copper have kept inventories relatively low. As the United States economy improves, the rise in copper demand and the need by consumers—i.e., manufacturers—to build inventories will cause copper prices to rise, possibly sharply as speculators fuel the rally. Unfortunately, sustained high levels of production by several major producing countries will eliminate any temporary shortage within a few months and lead to a drop in price, though probably not quite to prior lows.

It should be noted that this rather gloomy view is not universally held. One highly regarded Wall Street analyst has argued that prices will be considerably firmer than we anticipate in 1983 and 1984. If history is any guide, however, bear markets have tended to be deeper and longer than generally expected.

LME copper prices are expected to remain roughly in the range of 65–72 cents per pound through the remainder of 1982. Some improvement would be likely in 1983—to an average price of 78 cents under the most likely forecast and 70 cents under a less favorable environment. In either case, copper prices would be at unprofitable levels except for the most efficient producers.

The difference between the most likely and pessimistic forecasts becomes greater over time. In the most likely view, gradual improvement in the world economy eventually increases demand for copper sufficiently to draw down stocks. Moreover, few new mines will open during this period, while the buildup in weapons procurement in the United States could add significantly to copper demand. The result would be an average price of about $1.10 in 1985—still considerably below the 1980 price in real terms and well below our prior forecasts. Under the pessimistic forecast, the continued high levels of production by the LDCs would dominate all other factors and lead to a prolonged bear market for copper. This may not be the most likely possibility, but nevertheless it cannot be disregarded. Eventually—by 1986—under both scenarios a strong bull market would develop as increases in demand outpace supplies restrained by lack of new mine openings. In any case, it appears that boom-and-bust cycles in the copper market have been becoming more, rather than less, intense.

Index